Addiction and the Gospel

# Addiction *and the* Gospel

Jason Tackett

RESOURCE *Publications* · Eugene, Oregon

ADDICTION AND THE GOSPEL

Copyright © 2022 Jason Tackett. All rights reserved. Except for brief quotations in critical publications or reviews, no part of this book may be reproduced in any manner without prior written permission from the publisher. Write: Permissions, Wipf and Stock Publishers, 199 W. 8th Ave., Suite 3, Eugene, OR 97401.

Resource Publications
An Imprint of Wipf and Stock Publishers
199 W. 8th Ave., Suite 3
Eugene, OR 97401

www.wipfandstock.com

PAPERBACK ISBN: 978-1-6667-5297-7
HARDCOVER ISBN: 978-1-6667-5298-4
EBOOK ISBN: 978-1-6667-5299-1

08/22/22

All rights reserved. No portion of this book may be reproduced—mechanically, electronically, or by other means, including photocopying—without written permission of the author (Jason Tackett, West Liberty, KY—jason.tackett40@gmail.com).

All Scripture references use the King James Version of the Bible.

All reference used in regards to 12-step programs is found in the following reference:

*Alcoholics Anonymous: The Story of How Many Thousands of Men and Women Have Recovered from Alcoholism.* 4th ed. New York City: Alcoholics Anonymous World Services, 2001.

# Introduction

THIS SHORT TREATISE IS written for the many that the Lord has brought into my life struggling with drug and alcohol addiction. I share it knowing that the things contained therein will upset them, but they are yet true. I bless the day that my God sent people my way to speak these truths to me and I thereby was able to turn from my idols to the living God. I commend this to you with the conviction that I have spoken what is true and glorifying to my God. I ask that you prayerfully read it and look up the Scripture references. Examine yourself in the light of the Word of God. Victory can be found over all sin through Christ.

# Part 1: The Power Lacking in the Remedy of the World

"For what shall it profit a man, if he shall gain the whole world, and lose his own soul" (Mark 8:36)? It has been said that all medicine is poison and only has value when the therapeutic effect outweighs the harmful side effects (side effects being the direct effect of the poison). When it comes to an examination of drug and alcohol addiction treatments in general or 12-step programs in particular, one can admit to their therapeutic value. The 12-step programs are considered presently to be the gold standard in treatment of drug and alcohol addiction. There are some grumblings among the mental health community regarding the absence of individual therapy and the lack of empirical validity to the more spiritual aspects of the 12-steps. However, the suggested replacements for the 12-steps still incorporate the basic ideals of the 12-steps in their treatment. It is fiercely defended as the only means of maintaining sobriety by its participants and professionals within the substance abuse treatment system. It is hard to find a study or advocate that will speak disparagingly of these treatment programs. Therefore, there is often little discussion of its potential side effects.

One does not need to disagree with the whole of these treatment systems and see them as valueless in order to point out potential side effects. The 12-step programs lend themselves to a level of humility, a recognition of the possibility of a god above them and their need to seek a god, the need of making restitution for wrongs, the need of honesty, and a sense of charity and community. All of these are admittedly good things with great potential for therapeutic significance. However, if it helps someone on a therapeutic level to gain something loosely defined as sobriety and to gain some sense of a manageable daily life at the cost of devastating side effects, has it really helped? It has done partial good at the cost of great evil. If the side effect is to blind one to ultimate truth, to get them to trust in something less than the gospel, and to entrench them in a path leading to ultimate destruction, then all therapeutic value is destroyed. It is not truly medicinal, it is only poison. It does not really help, it only hurts. It becomes no different from the thing it professes to save one from. It becomes a source of escape from the greater problem hiding behind the thing we call addiction. If we create by our therapy a better-managed life destined for hell, we have failed to really help. We have failed in our ethical duty to do no harm. We are guilty of malpractice.

It is in this light that we begin to examine the potential side effects of drug and alcohol treatments in general and 12-step programs in specific. This will be done in the light of the Gospel of Christ, the Word of God, which is pure and right (Ps 19:7-10). The gospel is not medicine or treatment. It is free from truly harmful side effects. It is that which is truly life-altering or rather life-giving. All that speaks to the needs of mankind being met by sources other than the gospel must be immediately compared to the pure truth of the gospel in order to see their potential harm.

The best starting point with any discussion is what we actually know to be true. We cannot arrive at any conclusion by beginning with things that are unproven and untrustworthy. Therefore, for the Christian, we begin with the God of the Scriptures. We know that God is to be the one true God and that there are no other gods besides Him. We know that all things, especially all things in our lives and even our lives themselves, to be of Him, for Him, and to Him. The greatest purpose of our life is reflected in the first great commandment to love our God with all, to seek to know, rejoice in, honor, and glorify that God that is truly there.

We know further that we are sinners against that God and, due to our sin, we are separated from Him. It is only through the faith of Christ alone and the power of His Gospel that we are reconciled unto God from our sin. The gospel is central to the Christian. It alone is the power of God unto salvation (Rom 1:16). The gospel is not a work to perform, but a work completed by Christ on our behalf (1 Cor 15:1-10). While the wages of our sin is death, the gift of God is eternal life through Jesus Christ our Lord (Rom 6:23). The gospel is the truth that Christ died for our sins. He died taking our sin and our penalty upon Himself. He pled guilty for our sin and shame. Our sins were judged in Him. He did this in full accordance with the Scriptures that long expected His coming and His sacrifice. He was buried. He is risen again. He was declared to be the Son of God with power by the resurrection (Rom 1:4). This, again, was done in full accordance with the Scriptures. Finally, that risen Lord and Savior was seen of witnesses who declared His Gospel. We have the record of the Son of God given to us by God through those people that were His witnesses.

In the faith of Christ, we have all things that pertain to life and godliness (2 Pet 1:4). There is nothing that is lacking in the Gospel. All that we need to give us life and sustain our life is found in the faith of Christ. All that we need to live a godly life, in the will of God, is found in that record that God has given us. We marvel, therefore, that people who claim the name of Christ are so easily turned to another gospel (Gal 1:6-8). There is a great tragedy in the thought that someone may desire to forsake a fountain of living water for broken cisterns that can hold no water (Jer 2:3). The world is constantly offering alternatives to the Gospel of Christ, and those false gospels seem to be intuitive and good, but they lack true saving power. They offer the hearer something less than the fullness of Christ.

With that understanding as our backdrop, we now may enter into a full discussion of 12-step programs, which are considered the gold standard of treatment for drug and alcohol addiction in our culture. Since their development, they have promised recovery to people clutched by powerful addictions. The steps have now been incorporated into most forms of addiction treatments. The program presents an eclectic worldview of its own that makes it religious in nature (like all other views). It has its own view of morality, its own view of human nature, its own view of salvation, and so on. It has its own gospel that is spreading quickly across our landscape, as the treatment culture continues to grow. It has its own language and vernacular. When its adherents are presented with the faith of Christ, it stands in opposition to its proclaimed dogma. It becomes a stronghold in the minds of those that adopt it, keeping them from knowing the fullness of the truths of Christ.

The odd part is that churches have made claims that 12-step programs are congruent with the gospel and have attempted to incorporate them with their service to the addiction community. In order to do this, they must bend the intentions and imperatives of certain Scriptures to make it fit with the doctrines of 12-step theology. In doing so, they lose the power of the gospel and end up declaring to the world something less than the truths of Christ. They compromise the plain teaching of the Scriptures in order to embrace something that they have to repeatedly defend as being somewhat based on the Scriptures. One such advocate told me that they believed it was possible to be saved by Christ without believing anything to be true about Christ. They piously believed that the content of faith or the ability to believe certain points was not of saving value. This is contrary to the gospel that proclaims that one must believe upon Christ in order to be saved (Acts 16:31). Paul pointed out that salvation depends on hearing and believing that which is heard of Christ (Rom 10:13-17).

The 12-step program lends itself to such doctrinal bending. It is set up in such a way to allow it to co-op any religious tradition or doctrine it encounters, as long as that tradition or doctrine gives up on the idea that it is proclaiming any type of exclusivity. Jesus becomes *a* way instead of being *the* way. Being so malleable, it prevents itself from saying anything truly meaningful. There is a purposeful vagueness in 12-step treatments that shuts out all claims to truth. Trying to get the Bible to fit the program is dangerous. One must purposefully, or at least ignorantly, misinterpret the direct commands and indicatives of the Scriptures and embrace the vagueness.

## PART 1: THE POWER LACKING IN THE REMEDY OF THE WORLD

The true tragedy of Christian compromise is its transformation of the gospel itself. The gospel is the power of God (Rom 1:16). Those who receive it are given power to become children of God (John 1:12). The gospel has the power, when clearly declared, to save souls and change lives. The 12-step program usurps that claim and tells the addict that it alone has power to change his life. Its advocates often to speak the refrain, "it does not work, unless you work it." Unlike the gospel, which is a message to be believed, it offers instead a method to be practiced. To mesh the gospel with the 12-step program, the gospel must leave its place as a truth to be proclaimed to become a method to be worked.

The gospel becomes a form of treatment. It becomes no different from a form of continual therapy or a medical regimen, to be repeated over and over for the therapy of the patient, to make them feel like they by their effort are doing better. Whether we are talking about using the gospel to treat homosexuality or alcoholism, the gospel is not a treatment. It is not something added to other necessities. It is the only necessity for life and godliness. It is to be declared to the hearer without dilution, without coercion, and without mixture of worldly counsel or wisdom.

The myth that the vagueness of the 12-step claims is based on Scriptures is itself false. The program does adopt some biblical principles, such as the confession of faults and the making of restitution, but they do so while denying the whole of Scriptural truth. Bill Wilson, the founder of 12-step programs, was originally connected with a para-church organization known as the Oxford Group. They denied the need for formal Christian doctrine in favor of spiritual experience, which remains a core tenant of 12-step ideology. They preached the false gospel of moralism, telling people to do good and do right in order to work their own salvation through God. Doing moral works produced the spiritual experience of salvation.

Bill Wilson departed from the Oxford Group on the idea of power. They believed, contrary to the Scriptures (Rom 3:10-12), that each individual had power to do good. Bill believed that the drunkard was powerless over alcohol. Bill went on to create the

12-steps upon two unbiblical ideas. First, a medical doctor falsely told him that his drunkenness was a disease like an allergy and in no way a moral issue. Secondly, through the process of what he called spiritual enlightenment, he could maintain sobriety through the help of a power greater than himself. We will deal more directly in greater detail with these two deceptive errors shortly. For now, these two errors are the basis upon which all 12-step programs were built. Further, Bill Wilson claimed that he developed the 12 steps though spirit communication and not through the study of God's Word. This spiritual enlightenment included the use of hallucinogenic drugs and communication with spirits. Being developed on errors contradicting the Scriptures and developed out of a process that was outside of the scope of the Scriptures, the Christian should at least be willing to entertain the idea that the 12-step ideology may be the counsel of the ungodly (Ps 1:1). They must try the spirits to see if they are of God (1 John 4:1).

Why would we give up the Scriptures for something that is just claimed to be loosely based on the Scriptures? Why try to make the Scriptures, which are absolute truth, fit into something that is absent of those truths? These steps are not based on the Scriptures at all. They are based on modern psychology or biological and social determinism. They are not built on the idea of the soul being responsible to God for its works. It is actually based on a faulty view of salvation (working the steps) and not on salvation received from God by grace without merit. It is based on a replacement for the gospel as the means of salvation. It is based on a denial of the reality of sin. The Christian should beware of giving ear to worldly philosophical systems, which draw us away from Christ (Col 2:8).

It may be claimed that the program works. However, pragmatism is not synonymous with truth. Just because something is effective in one way does not mean it is true. I had one program leader once tell me that if he could get someone to believe that a chair was their higher power, then he could get them to maintain sobriety. Well, what advantage is there in all areas of life for that person to believe a chair was his high power? Further, to say one

## PART 1: THE POWER LACKING IN THE REMEDY OF THE WORLD

should seek a higher power for help may be just as satanic as it is Christian. Satan, after all, is a higher power. There are other spirits with power that could help, especially if it led away from Christ-centered worship. However, these other sources of greater power are not of the truth.

There is something worse than struggling with alcohol or drug addiction. One may save their life in one sense at the expense of losing it in the ultimate sense (Matt 16:25). To bring a person to a point that they deny the very truths, which alone could affect their eternal salvation, is a far worse thing. A 12-step program may or may not help a person get sober and stay sober. One does not really know if it does. However, even if it does, if it hardens the heart against Christ, it has not really helped that person. What shall it profit a man if he gains sobriety and loses his own soul (Mark 8:36).

If the process of getting sober creates a stronghold against the gospel, then the process of getting sober does not work. The gospel can give victory over sin. Other things may treat the symptoms of sin. Nevertheless, what man truly needs is the gospel. There is a danger in treatment of symptoms over the addressing of the cause. People seek drugs and alcohol because they are sinners. There is only one answer for sin. Who can forgive sins but God (Mark 2:5-11)? Sins can only be forgiven through Christ. The lack of a pill does not make one sick. The lack of a 12-step program does not cause alcoholism. Alcohol and drug uses are the fruit and sin is the root. The 12-steps cannot address the real need. Christ alone is the answer for sin.

The cost of embracing 12-step theology is too high. You must trade true riches for paper currency backed by nothing. While it may provide a season of relief, it cannot bring true lasting change. It may give a mechanism for temporary sobriety, but it cannot give eternal life. Instead, it reinforces ideas contrary to the truths that can bring lasting change and eternal life. Consider the following tradeoffs demanded by the 12-step program.

# Tradeoff # 1

FIRST, ONE MUST TRADE *the most High God for a higher power.* The first command must be broken in order to embrace the steps. We are commanded to not have any other gods before Him (Exod 20:3). Further, the greatest commandment is that we are to love God with all that we have and all we are (Matt 22:36). We cannot love Him with all while proclaiming that God is something less than He truly is or telling others that they have our blessing in doing so. We cannot make God something less than He is without creating a new god or idol after our own image. God said this, ". . .thou thoughtest that I was altogether such an one as thyself: but I will reprove thee, and set them in order before thine eyes. Now consider this, ye that forget God, lest I tear you in pieces, and there be none to deliver" (Ps 50:21, 22). He went on to say, "Whoso offereth praise glorifieth me: and to him that ordereth his conversation aright will I shew the salvation of God" (Ps 50:23). The danger of embracing a god of your own understanding and a higher power is that one is creating an idol. They limit the Most High God to the boundaries of their own understanding. This is exactly what the 12-steps ask of its adherents, "choose your own conception of God." Even if one claims that they are using that language for the sake of the others in the program, they are failing to offer true praise and allowing the perpetuation of idol worship. This is not a system that honors the one true God.

When the 12-step program uses the word *God*, it is not the God of the Scriptures. The god of the 12-steps is defined by man and not revealed to man. This god is limited to the understanding of people. The God of the Scriptures is defined by Himself and revealed to us through Christ (John 1:18).

*The Serenity Prayer* is the closest anyone in a 12-step meeting will come to engaging or acknowledging a god openly. It is an internal part of each 12-step meeting and gives a semblance of collective worship. The version of the 12-steps is purposefully stripped of any language of God as the heavenly Father or any mention of Jesus Christ as the Son of God, as earlier versions of the prayer contained. The 12-step version is as follows:

> God, grant me the serenity to accept the things I cannot change, courage to change the things I can, and wisdom to know the difference.

When compared with the model prayer of Christ, the anemic nature of the prayer is seen.

> "Our Father which art in heaven, Hallowed be thy name. Thy kingdom come, Thy will be done in earth, as it is in heaven. Give us this day our daily bread. And forgive us our debts, as we forgive our debtors. And lead us not into temptation, but deliver us from evil: For thine is the kingdom, and the power, and the glory, for ever. Amen" (Matt. 6:9-13).

In the 12-step prayer, there is no recognition of the exalted position of God or His name, that which He revealed Himself to be. There is no longing for His rule or submission to His will. There is no statement of dependency on God or humility before Him as a sinner (see Luke 11:4). There is no concern in the prayer for His leadership. It does not attempt to attribute glory to the one true God. The petitions in the 12-step prayer are not evil, but absent the vital elements of the model prayer, they become man-centered and shut out the glory of God. To limit your prayer life to requests that you may have personal peace about circumstances in your life is to fail to have a prayer life after the will of the holy and just God.

The nature of God is transcendent and demands humility and fear. This is not recognized in the rooms of Alcoholics Anonymous (AA) and Narcotics Anonymous (NA). Settling only for a god that is bound by their own understanding, all their religious experience fails to reach out to the Most High. It ignores the fact that this God has made Himself known. "The Lord thundered from heaven, and the most High uttered his voice" (2 Sam 22:14). In

## PART 1: THE POWER LACKING IN THE REMEDY OF THE WORLD

addition, it is only the mercy of the Most High that can affect real recovery or victory. "For the king trusteth in the Lord, and through the mercy of the most High he shall not be moved" (Ps 21:7). The world knows the eternal power and Godhead of the Most High, His judgement and wrath; therefore, they prefer to make a God after the image of man (Rom 1). They do not want a God that is beyond their thoughts. "For as the heavens are higher than the earth, so are my ways higher than your ways, and my thoughts than your thoughts" (Isa 55:9). However, only such a God is worthy of worship, and the ignoring of such a God is worthy of judgement and wrath. "For the Lord most high is terrible; he is a great King over all the earth" (Ps 47:2). To sin against the light of the knowledge of the Most High, to not see Him as He has revealed Himself to be, the Ruler of all things worthy of all our worship, is to bring a sure destruction upon our heads (Dan 5:18-30).

We have been warned of God to lean not to our own understanding but to acknowledge Him in all our ways (Prov 3:5, 6). There are none that understand and seek God (Rom 3:10-12). That is the depraved nature of humanity. The steps deny that truth and begin with the idea that man can understand and seek God. This is false. Therefore, our understanding of God cannot get us to God. Bill Wilson stated that he felt liberated when he heard that he could create his own conception of God. However, we do not have the ability or the right to define God. God alone can and does define Himself, and we honor Him alone by believing Him. He is light, self-revealing, and we are to walk in the light He has given (2 John 1:4-7). It is our sin alone that keeps us from walking in that light (John 3:19-21).

The god of 12-step programs resembles more of pagan idolatry than genuine worship of the one true God. The idols of paganism were always localized to a particular area of life. They would seek one idol to help with the harvest and another to help with love and child bearing and yet another to ward off sickness. All of this was a denial of the one true God that unifies all of existence. For the addict, they are presented with a god that can help them with their addiction, but need not be involved in any other part of their life. The last step they take does ask them to apply the steps to all areas of their life, but this does not necessitate any desire after God. In fact, the spiritual awakening comes from the steps and not from God and it is to the steps, and their own effort in taking the steps, that they owe allegiance. The steps themselves become their god. In addition, the god that they speak of is just a tool to use to get a desired end. It is a tool just like things in the other steps: the moral inventory, the confession, restitution, and giving back. The Most High is not a tool to use but a being to be worshipped and adored.

Those that engage in the 12-steps can claim to be spiritual without holding any faith or devotion to God that demands anything of them in all aspects of their life. The will of their god is limited to their understanding and the will of that god is contained in the steps. The cycle of the steps is seeing yourself powerless and in constant need of the steps and the meetings that perpetuate them. I often hear people speak of needing a meeting when they have a bad day. It is a popular idea that God is always there when I need Him, but there is no need for that God to have a vital daily relationship with me. God is, in such a scenario, like a tow truck driver. I can call Him to get me out of trouble and then there is no further need of Him. This is far from the God of the Scriptures of which all things are of Him, through Him, and to Him (Rom 11:33-36).

Such a god, as created by the 12-steps, is only of pragmatic value. Such a god has no real saving efficacy. Such a god is unworthy of any real worship. Ultimately, those who trade the one true God for this idol, created by their own understanding, are trusting in a god that is sure to fail. Grace and peace come only from the one true God (Rom 1:7, 1 Cor 1:3, 2 Cor 1:2, Gal 1:3). Ultimate victory comes only through the one true God. "O my God, I trust in thee: let me not be ashamed, let not mine enemies triumph over me" (Ps 25:2). "For thou, Lord, hast made me glad through thy work: I will triumph in the works of thy hands" (Ps 92:4). "Now thanks be unto God, which always causeth us to triumph in Christ, and maketh manifest the savour of his knowledge by us in every place" (2 Cor 2:14). It is a vain hope to look for victory in something less than the God that truly is. The need is not for something higher but for the Most High.

# Tradeoff # 2

SECONDLY, ONE MUST TRADE *the reality of sin for the mirage of addiction*. The whole of the gospel of recovery (Gal 1:6-9) that is proclaimed by the 12-steps is built on a foundation that addiction is a disease of which the addict has no control and no moral responsibility in its perpetuation. That is always specifically, what is meant when they speak of being powerless. The rooms of AA and NA have not moved from these foundational ideas. They are aided and abetted by the contemporary psychological community, which has reduced the individual human to a strictly material existence and wholly determined in all things by the chemical makeup and reactions in their brain. Behind this materialistic philosophy is a denial of the reality of God and the soul and all moral responsibility of the soul to God. If there is no soul, or immaterial reality in man, then there is no ability for man to act freely above the material world of cause and effect. Therefore, all God talk that is used after this fact comes from an ideology that stands contrary to the truth of God and stands contrary to the view of man as a free moral agent responsible to God (Rom 14:12). It is no wonder that the word *sin* is absent from the rooms of AA and NA.

    The term *addiction* is not, in those rooms, a word that speaks of an acquired habit or compulsive activity that someone has developed as a consequence of their own past choices or other environmental conditions. If so, the Christian would likely agree with them. Now addiction is not in itself bad, one can develop good compulsions and habitual behaviors (2 Cor 16:15). Addiction, according to the steps, is rather defined as a treatable and chronic medical disease. It is aggravated by personal choice and environment, but is based in the chemical makeup of the brain circuits and genetics. The activity one is addicted to is considered amoral, neither right nor wrong. Other people can do it without any ramifications who do not suffer from the disease of addiction. However, the addict is the one that engages in the behavior compulsively despite harmful consequences. There is no medical test that can diagnose this disease, and it is only inferred based on harmful behavior that follows. Even if there is harmful behavior present or if that person is able to quit their drug and alcohol use without the use of treatment, then it is deemed of that person that they were not truly an addict. Therefore, the diagnosis of addiction is arbitrary and unscientific. One is only truly an addict if one needs treatment, specifically that treatment provided by the 12-steps. They remain addicts for the rest of their lives without possibility of final victory. There is no other valid way to diagnose it as one would other medical diseases like cancer.

In addition, addiction being a disease, one is not morally responsible for the development and continuance of the compulsive behavior. The underlying message of the 12-steps is one of moral passivity in all decisions to begin the use of substances or continue in that use. Even continued use while in treatment is an amoral thing, an inevitable relapse deemed to be a part of treatment and not a choice to sin. There is, in the rooms of AA and NA, no underlying independent lust or selfish and sinful desire behind those choices that may be called sinful. We would not blame the cancer patient for the development and progress of their cancer. This is a denial of the real and substantial existence of sin and the guilt of sin. As such, it attempts to cover the sinfulness of their addiction and keeps them from ever truly knowing victory. "He that covereth his sins shall not prosper: but whoso confesseth and forsaketh them shall have mercy" (Prov 28:13).

The moral activity of getting drunk and doing drugs, and the compulsion one develops to live a life defined by those activities, is reduced to that like an allergy to pollen one is born with, reacts to, and for which one has no moral responsibility. One breathes in pollen and it causes sneezing. One is exposed to alcohol and it causes their life to be out of control. They are powerless and not morally responsible for the allergic reaction. They conclude that it is not therefore a sin. This ideology has produced a myriad of spin offs covering all manner of sin under the same disease model. There is now 12-step programs for sex addicts (excusing sexual immorality), anger, overeaters (excusing the sin of gluttony), gamblers, shopaholics, debtors (all excusing, as a disease, the sin of covetousness), and many other such. The embracing of this addiction model is the embracing of an ideology that excuses all manner of sin. No amount of talk about moral accounting and the need to take a fierce moral inventory within the steps rescues the steps from this rotten foundation.

The Christian has no issues with the idea that a person has a predisposition toward things that are evil. Men love darkness rather than light because their deeds are evil (John 3:19). Men are victims of the first choice of man to sin (Rom 5:12). Mankind has fallen from God and is totally depraved. They cannot do good works toward God. They are powerless in the sense of being reconciled to God. They are unable to make one move toward God in their lost state; and therefore, their salvation had to be fully affected by Christ. They were without strength to affect anything as to their salvation (Rom 5:8-11). That powerlessness does not negate their ability to make choices or their real moral responsibility for those choices. They are victims of the first choice to sin, but they are also violators. They have freely chosen to do wrong, knowing it to be wrong. They are guilty and deserving of judgement (Rom 3:19, 20). When we remove the reality of sin, we take away that which can show them their need for Christ. Christ died for sins. Christ came to save sinners (1 Tim 1:15). Leaving out the reality of sin leaves them without the possibility of knowing the Savior. It is not an allergy. It is sin. One day they will stand before Christ, and the books will be open (Rev 20:11-15). They will be guilty and without excuse. There is a danger in the omission of the subject of sin.

This is the natural bent of all lost people. Each human being is naturally rebellious against God and naturally bent toward evil and its modes of worship. We do not teach babies to lie. They know naturally how to lie. There is a potentiality of evil in all. If a toddler wanted a toy and had the strength of an adult, it would kill to get it. We are not basically good and fall into evil, but we are basically evil and have to strive to do good. Moreover, we are morally responsible to strive. That does not mean that each individual human is as evil as possible. What it does mean is that mankind is naturally drawn to sin and is unable to come to God or do that which is truly good apart from God. As such, they do all manner of evil things (Rom 1-3). Each man is a sinner that loves, in their own way, to do evil works. Nevertheless, they are morally responsible and will be judged for their works.

Alcohol and drug use is just one of many sinful choices that sinful men make. They are not predetermined by God to commit any specific sin. God is not the author of their sin but rather their own heart and their own lust (Matt 15:18-20, Jas 1:13-15). Where does all of the vileness of the sin of drunkenness come from? If it was not already in you, how could the state of intoxication ever bring it out of you? There is nothing inherent in that object that hates, steals, or destroys others. That all is in you and the drug and alcohol created the occasion to bring it out. It uninhibited you. It comes from you, and the things in your heart and desires. Moreover, God is just to judge those sins. The idea that the choice to use and misuse/abuse substances in search of a pleasure for your own flesh is not a sin for which people will be rightly judged is an idea foreign to the Scriptures and moral reasoning. As such, drunkenness is not a disease but a worship disorder. When we see it, we see someone actively rebelling against the Most High. We are seeing someone who has set themselves up as their own god. When we hear of the drunk beating their spouse, robbing houses, and crashing fatally into unsuspecting victims, we are hearing the sound of worship. All the effects of drunkenness are the fruit of man worshipping their false gods.

To deny the idea of sin, in favor of the disease model, is to make us something less than human. It is to reduce us to the instinctual behavior of animals, controlled by stimulus and response. It is to deny that we are moral creatures with dignity in favor of an idea that we are amoral creatures without an ability to act above our base nature. What is worse, it offers as the only redemptive work from that powerlessness a spiritual awakening provided by the steps. Again, talk of making a fierce moral inventory cannot rescue such a system from its base denial of morality. If your drunkenness is not a moral failing, then neither is anything else you may find in a moral inventory. All can be excused with the disease model.

The object that the addict (the sinner) seeks is sinful and to seek it is to transgress the law of God. The sin of choosing those things reveals that they have a heart against God. This does not need to spiral into a debate of whether social drinking or the occasional use of fermented drinks is acceptable. Those who seek alcohol and drugs, those relevant to our discussion, do so because they desire an altered state of consciousness, a state of drunkenness. God has told us, "Be not drunk with wine . . . " (Eph 5:18). It is pleasing to the flesh and the senses; it is self-edifying. That is why people seek it, regardless of how it damages people around them. It is sinful.

They are called spirits. They affect one spiritually. They have an influence over people that give themselves over to them. They are idols. They are devils. Bacchus, the god of drunkenness and reveling, was a false god, an idol. We are to turn to God from idols (1 Thess 1:9, 1 John 5:21). When we approach drunkenness, we are approaching a powerful personal influence, and we enter into an act of worship. Wine is a mocker and those who are deceived by it lack wisdom (Prov 20:1). It is a deceiving thing, a personal influence, to lure people after its pseudo-shiny rewards. It is a work of the flesh that is contrary to the work of the Spirit of God (Gal 5:19-21). It is kin to the sin of gluttony (Prov 23:21). We are beseeched to not even look at the fermented wine, when it is pleasing in its advertising (Prov 23:29-35, it brings with it foolish bondage to seek it again, as well as perverse speech and sexual immorality). It is a sin to set strong drink before our neighbor to make them drunk (Hab 2:15). It is connected to the sin of pride (Isa 28:1-3). Christ connected it with the sin of the unfaithful servant (Matt 24:49). One can claim that Christ made water into wine, but none can say that He set a strong drink before

His neighbor or declared it a righteous thing to be drunk. It is a sin to be avoided for those who know Christ (Rom 13:13). It is a sin that, among many others, if it defines one's character, is indicative of being lost and without Christ (2 Cor 5:11, 6:11, 12). This includes all substances that bring a person under its influence and alters their state of consciousness. The command of the Scriptures is to be sober (2 Pet 5:8). For someone to say that this is a disease and not a moral choice is an affront to the commands and principles of the Scriptures.

The Christian maintains that the act of becoming drunk occurs in the context of God's moral imperatives and commands, which all men are free to choose and morally responsible to reject that which is contrary to them. Drunkenness is a sin. It is not a disease in the sense of being beyond the moral responsibility of man toward God. This stands in direct opposition to the underlying teaching of the 12-steps. The Christian does not deny the idea that the particular sin of drunkenness may be more besetting to some people than it is of others. The besetting sin of some men is pride and self-righteousness. The besetting sin of others is the lust of the flesh. Others may struggle with covetousness. The root of all sin is unbelief and rebellion against God. It is the fear of God that compels us to depart from iniquity (Prov 16:6). Our first parents sinned because they did not believe God or fear Him. We rebel against God because of the same factors. They did not sin because of genetics or environment, for theirs were perfect. Those things may have complicated our situation, but it is unbelief and lack of fear that is at the bottom of our sin too. It does not take another addict to understand an addict. The root of all is sin. The Christian can understand sin and more importantly salvation from sin. The sin of drunkenness may not be the full expression of sin in many. As such, they may appear to be able to "drink responsibly" and leave the strong drink alone. Others, however, will find the feeling of intoxication so enjoyable that they will chase that pleasure to harmful excesses.

There are two biblical ideas that may make this disposition of some toward drunkenness a more apparent sinful expression than it may appear in others. The first is the idea of familial curses. God has proclaimed that he will visit the sins of the father upon the children to the third and fourth generation (Exod 20:5, 34:7). This does not deny the existence of choice, but is a judgment upon the children of one who chooses sin (Deut 30:19). We have the ability to pass blessings down to our children by doing that which is righteous, and we have the ability to pass curses down upon our children by our wrong choices. The natural bent of the children is to follow the deeds of their parents. The principle is that we train our children in the way they should go and when they are older, they will not depart from that way (Prov 22:6). This should heighten us to the responsibility that we have to do right. If we give ourselves over to drunkenness, we increase the chances that our children will follow us into that curse. Familial culture is such a powerful influence on the following generations that it is difficult for that culture to be broken from it. Even in the case of absent parents, it is often an observable phenomenon to see the children do the deeds of their parents. Your choices have consequences, not just for you but also for those that follow you

This, however, is not the same as saying that our biology is our destiny. When they speak of being powerless biology is destiny is what they mean, not the doctrine of depravity or judgement. Again, we are victims of sin, but not in the sense of the disease model. We are victims of the decisions of our fathers, chiefly Adam. We are children of disobedience and wrath (Eph 2:2, 3). We are by nature sinners. However, we still freely choose sin based on our own lusts. We are violators of God's law by choice, our consciences bearing witness. We love them and pursue them, even to our own death (Prov 11:19, 1 Pet 4:3). We chose our sins. Despite the powerful influence of familial culture, each person is still responsible before God to choose right. The disease model makes one an absolute slave to their genetics and denies the moral responsibility of man. The disease model adopts the Jewish proverb that our fathers have eaten sour grapes and now our teeth are set on edge, a proverb that God said He despised (Ezek 18:2). Ezekiel, in that context, went on to refute that idea by examining three generations of men who were responsible to God alone for their actions. He told of a king that did evil who had a son that saw all that evil and turned from it. That king who chose right had a son that rejected all that was right and chose instead to follow sin. The declaration of God was that the father would not die for the son's sin, nor the son for the father's sin. Each man is responsible to God for his own works. Each man will die for his own sins (Ezek 18:3, 4). Each person will be judged for deeds that they chose to do in their body, regardless of the context and environment in which they lived.

The second biblical idea, which lends credence to the idea that some find the abuse of substance to be more besetting than others, is the idea of the bondage of sin itself. All of humanity is sinful and each person has his or her compulsions to some form of sin. Just because the "addict" runs after their sin despite its dire consequences in their life does not make their expression of sin any different from others. All sin is unto death. When we give in to our lust, it brings forth sin, which always ends in death (Jas 1:13-15). The judgment on drunkenness is just more apparent. Others appear only on the surface to be happy in their sin without those immediate and observable dire consequences. Nevertheless, those consequences will come. One preacher gave the example of the polar bear. The Eskimo had a unique way of killing polar bears, other than attempting to fight them directly. They would kill a seal and freeze it with a sharp blade under its skin. The bear would smell the blood and come after the seal. The bear in its appetite would begin to eat the seal and lap up its blood, not realizing its initial injuries and continuing despite them. In its lust, it continues to lap up the blood of the seal and its own blood until it collapses from loss of blood. That is an apt picture of the addict, and all sinners, pursuing sin unto their own death (Prov 11:19).

With that being said, the Christian will admit that there is an obvious compulsion to those who have given themselves over to the sin of drunkenness. The Christian does not define this as a disease but as sin brought forth by one's own lust. The reason for the compulsion to drink is that sin results in bondage and death. Sin enslaves people. The promise of alcohol and drugs is that it will set you free. It will let you escape your problems and anxieties. It will release you from your inhibitions. It will give you peace and open the doors of your perception. It will free you from whatever is weighing you down. It will bring you happiness. Therefore, they ignore the commands and warnings of Scripture and choose to sin. Once overcome by the sin, they are stuck in the constant chase for those illusive promises of liberty. Being overcome with sin, they find themselves in bondage (2 Pet 2:19). It becomes the defining point of their character. They become servants to their sin. We become the servant or slave of the things we yield to (Rom 6:16). This is not the product of the outworking of a disease but the product of choice and rebellion against God in favor of a god they chose. We willingly chase after sin to find ourselves in the end unable to free ourselves from its clutches. There are powers that seek to bring us under their rule (2 Cor 6:12).

Despite the reality of familial influence and spiritual bondage, the reality of drunkenness is that it is sin. You do it because you desire it, and you like what it does for you. It serves your flesh. You may sorrow and despair over how it affects the rest of your life, but you still run after it because you like what it does for you in your selfishness. It is sinful, we will speak further of the evil of this sin later. Each person that engages in this sin, whether they develop a compulsion to it or not, is responsible to God for their choice to sin. They incur real and true guilt, which must be brought into account (Rom 14:12). We are sinners in Adam, but still guilty in our own lusts. The denial that it is a sin fails to account for the real and substantial guilt of it. It attempts to cover the sin with the fig leaves of disease, as Adam did in the Garden of Eden. It attempts to shift the blame away from themselves to their parents or their environment. This pushes them further away from the real answer to their problem, repentance toward the Most High God from their sin. Again, anyone who covers their sin will not prosper (Prov 28:13). God wants us to see ourselves as sinners, both as victims in need of rescue and violators in need of forgiveness. He wants us to see ourselves as desperately needing Him and powerless only in the sense of being unable to get to Him. He wants us to see the exceeding sinfulness of our sin so we can see the glory of His salvation. The steps want us to be only victims and not violators so we seek treatment and not forgiveness and atonement.

# Tradeoff # 3

THIRDLY, ONE MUST TRADE *trust in the gospel of Christ for working the steps*. This is a diabolical trade that plays to the flesh of men. The gospel saves based on grace through faith. It is received as a free gift. Moreover, the receiving of it is a life-altering experience that influences all areas of one's life. It produces a new life, a new birth, a new creation, with new affections and direction for one's life. Those who encounter the message of the gospel are changed thereby. The tradeoff then is to replace the message with a method, to trade the one who is *the* Way for *a* way that seems right to men (Prov 14:12).

The idiom of the AA and NA rooms is that in order to begin to recover from alcohol or drug abuse one must "work the steps." Working the steps is synonymous with delivering one from the bondage of what they deny to be sin and it is the means according to the last step of achieving a life changing spiritual awakening. Whereas the Scriptures teach that one is dead in sins and quickened only by the grace of God (Eph 2:1-10), the steps teach "a spiritual awakening . . . . [is] the result of these Steps." Regardless of the denial of the truth of sin, this is an obvious works-based salvation. As such, it stands completely opposed to the grace-based message of the gospel of Christ. It is a prescriptive outline of hoops one must jump through, and keep jumping through, in order to have and maintain victory from sin. It clearly teaches that through the working of the steps one can awaken or regenerate one's self with only nominal help from God. This is a denial of the scriptural doctrine of total depravity and grace. It is, at its base, a self-help program, a program of self-improvement that relies wholly on the power of self to effect change. God is a tool used in working this change, that is a god that is defined by the self, limited to the thoughts of the self, and only possessing powers that are defined

## TRADEOFF # 3

by the self. It is no different from the modern evangelical outreach, pressing the need for decisions and repeated prayers on converts, declaring that by doing such things change occurs. This is opposed to grace that sees salvation as wholly of God, a supernatural event in which God on the basis of grace without works gives mercy to the sinner, gives life from the dead.

This is where the language of the 12-steps becomes deceptive. Many of its adherents will talk about a real change of heart, but it is a change of heart brought about by AA and not by Christ. The steps themselves appear to talk about many good things such as handing one's will over to God (not necessarily the Most High God), making a moral inventory of ourselves and confessing our faults, reconciling with those whom we have wronged, and so on. The bottom line is that the steps are steps that are taken by people with the promise that if they take those steps that those steps themselves will change their life. It is a statement of faith in something to save. They remain lost in an endless cycle of a process salvation. Hence, they can never speak of being recovered, but only in recovery. They can maintain that "once an addict, always an addict" and can never speak of all things becoming new (2 Cor 5:17). They cannot say they were once lost, but now are found (1 Cor 6:9-11). Salvation begins and continues without end for them when they decide to admit that they are powerless (which means they are not morally responsible for their addiction), when they look for a higher power (which does not need to be the Most High God of revelation), when they turn their lives over to a higher power, when they make a moral inventory, when they confess their wrongs, when they are ready to allow their higher power to remove their defects, when they ask to be made better, when they make a list of their offended and show willingness to make amends, when they make amends, when they continue in what they have learned, when they seek God in prayer, when they begin to carry the message of the 12-steps, and when they spend the rest of their lives repeating the same steps.

Much of this, at least in summary form, is good advice for things one should strive to do. There are, though, several problems with the steps. Mostly, they lack any recognition of anything done by God. One could replace all mention of God with a can opener or a fried egg and the steps would still remain the same. They are nothing more than a list of things for the individual to perform. God is incidental to the whole thing. There is an underlying assumption that, however one decided to define God, God will simply play along with the whole scheme. There is a pride at the bottom of all of this. There is no fear of God, nor any recognition that we need to be reconciled to God because of our sin. There is no realization that one stands subject to the wrath of God and therefore they should cry out to God for mercy. There is no recognition that God decides on whom He will have mercy (Rom 9:15-28), and therefore no sense of urgency to cry out to God for mercy. God is under no obligation to save anyone and every sinner should come to God with a humility reflecting that fearful truth. God is not what the steps perceive Him to be. The Most High God is not playing along with man's schemes. The steps see God as a puppet to be used in the scheme of their self-improvement program.

Neutered of the holy and just God and the idea of sin, one is left with a list of things for someone to do, decide to do, or be willing to do in order to get and maintain sobriety. One may give lip service to "accepting spiritual help," but they do so behind the backdrop of being "willing to make the effort." The Scriptures however proclaim that salvation is not of works, but by grace through faith (Eph 2:8, 9). Grace and works do not mix (Rom 11:5, 6). The popular phraseology for those in treatment is that they are "working the steps" and that is what they are encouraged over and over to do. Working the steps is all that they have to offer for salvation from that particular sin. And once they stop working the steps, the self-fulfilling prophecy comes true, they lose that salvation in what they call relapse. They start back at zero. There is no rest from the work that one would experience in Christ (Matt 11:28). There is no security in grace as promised in Christ (1 Pet 1:5).

The steps begin with your work and your work alone. They continue with your work and your work alone. They end in your work and your work alone. There is only lip service to dependency

## TRADEOFF # 3

upon God. One constantly hears in the treatment community wordly-wise phrases like, "pray like everything depends on God, but act like everything depends on you," and "fake it 'til you make it." Such phraseology betrays dependency upon self. When this becomes the sum total of your standing before God, then you will differ nothing from Cain who thought that he would be accepted by God based on the fruit of his own labor. It is to fail to attain the true faith of Abel, who knew that the work of his hands could not make him righteous before God. Abel brought the blood of a substitute, the blood of one that died for him in his place. One must trust in Him who did all the work for salvation for them.

To begin with the idea that one is powerless against a particular sin and then to prescribe 11 more steps to do in their own power is a contradiction. Further, it misses the real truth of your condition. You are not powerless against sin; you are powerless in the matter of salvation. You cannot get to God due to your sins based on your own effort. All the determinations you make will not move you one inch closer to salvation. All the steps toward sobriety that you take only leave you lost and under the judgement and wrath of God as a sinner. You stand in need of mercy and making decisions to do certain things cannot get that mercy to you. You need to seek mercy from the one true God. You need the merit of one that was without sin (2 Cor 5:21). You need the Gospel of Christ who cried, "It is finished," when He died for you.

The answer to the question of what must I do to be saved is to believe on Jesus Christ (Acts 16:31). A true fearless moral inventory would discover your moral bankruptcy and would lead you to see that you are "guilty of all" (Jas 2:10). The steps tell you that you do have power to save yourself, no matter what verbiage they scatter through their steps. They speak nothing of your guilt before God and need of repentance. They offer you a method. Christianity offers you a message, something to be believed and trusted, a life-changing message to all who hear the good news. It is done in Christ. God is rich in mercy. We can find new life in Him alone. Christ is the only way. Every sinner that comes to Him, He saves. Every sinner He saves, He keeps (John 6:37). There is mercy to be had for all who trust alone in Christ and not in their own righteousness. Ye must be born again by trusting Christ (John 3:3, 5, 14-16). The difference between the steps and the faith of Christ are the differences between a dead man trying to be moral and one being raised to new life in Christ. It is not of works (Eph 2:8, 9).

# Tradeoff # 4

THEN, ONE MUST TRADE *the Holy Scriptures for the Big Book.* Everything always boils down to the question of authority. What we do is based on what we believe, which is based on who we choose to believe (1 John 5:9-12). It boils down to the question, "who says?" Who do we believe and who will we allow to shape our behavior? In this sense, every faith has a sacred text, some written and some unwritten. All forms of drug treatment have a sacred text. For the more sterile forms of treatment, the sacred text is the authority of the psychologist or the psychological system. The Big Book is the sacred text of the 12-step programs. No one will talk about it as sacred, but it is integral to their engagement in treatment, their understanding of the steps and traditions, and to their having a common agreed on authority in their treatment. Many in the program know it as the book of experience. It introduces the steps and traditions of the program and offers testimonial experiences of those who have worked the steps. Its purpose is to connect the current participant in the program with a community of real addicts across space and time. Within the text itself, there is a denial that others who have, through other means, left alcohol without the program are real alcoholics or addicts. Knowing that most people who engage in the activity of drugs and alcohol will quit at some point on their own without the aid of a program, it identifies such only as social drinkers or strong drinkers and not real alcoholics like themselves. For the real alcoholic, there is only hope in the community and steps presented to them in the Big Book. The Big Book therefore is that thing that links the individual to the community. In and of itself, this is not necessarily a bad thing. However, the doctrinal absence of the Most High God and the reality of sin that it perpetuates is already problematic, as we have seen.

## PART 1: THE POWER LACKING IN THE REMEDY OF THE WORLD

We will deal shortly with a comparison of the community of believers and the community offered by the steps. Here, we attempt only to see the superiority of the Scriptures to the text of the Big Book. I have personally met many in the program that attempted to put the two on the same level. Even if they do not do so verbally, they will put more emphasis on studying and applying the principles of the Big Book and ignore the Scriptures, unless they can be made to mesh with the Big Book. I met one individual that attempted to say that the Big Book is an extension of the experiences of a community seeking God just like the Bible. The basis of that belief is postmodern. It denies that there is absolute truth that transcends the boundaries of the community, truth is determined by the community and not the community being shaped and defined by their relationship to independent truth. To see the apostolic authority of the Scriptures in such a light is damnable and is to deny the reality of Christ. To see the Big Book as an extension of the same authority of the community of faith is to untether us from truth. If the Scriptures are true, all that contradicts their tenants is false. The Big Book and the Scriptures do not share the same authority of faith. When we speak of the faith of Christ, we are speaking of revealed truths that we trust and not the subjective experience of any believer. It is the words of Christ being believed and lived. That truth alone can make us free (John 8:31, 32).

Most extra-biblical cults start with the same assumption; the Book of Mormon is claimed to be an extension of the same authority of the Scriptures, as does the Koran. Christ and His gospel and all the prophetic utterances that create the backdrop of the gospel have demonstrated the Scriptures to be true. No such verification exists for any extra-biblical texts, all of which deny the basic tenets of the gospel; including the Big Book. There is a difference between the Scriptures and the ramblings of Jim Jones, who murdered 900 of his followers. They did not arise from the same authority. While that is an outrageous comparison, the same principle applies to all other texts that exist. There is a big difference between Bill Wilson, who taught that we can create our own conception of God and denied the reality of sin, and Christ who is the true revelation of the true God (Heb 1:1-3). The testimony of the Most High is that we hear Christ (Matt 17:5).

The Big Book, when compared with the Scriptures, does not offer us anything else but the words and fallible opinions of the minds of men. That does not mean that there is no value in the book, just that we cannot approach it with the same sense of confidence. We apply that to all other forms of treatment. The psychologist may have a lot of good insight, but has no absolute authority. We need absolute authority, and we should seek it among all the voices that speak. This then is the question; does the wisdom come from a true authority or a fallible source?

The Bible is not simply a book to be read and obeyed. It is not a chronicle of subjective experiences of arbitrary belief. It is a point of contact between us and the eternal God who has made Himself known in history. If I read Shakespeare, I only get to know the thoughts of Shakespeare. However, when I read the Scriptures, I get to know the mind of God. Behind every text of the Scriptures, there is a God that I can know in a better and more joyful way. Each verse contains Christ, and I can there love and rejoice in Him as I learn to follow Him closer. The Bible is not a long list of external demands on our life, but rather it is holy ground where we can worship the one true God as He reveals Himself to us.

When we read the Big Book, we read only the mind of the AA founder and people who followed him. They are fallible and finite, just like us. We read the words of one that has denied the true existence of the Most High God in favor of a god chosen after one's own perception and understanding. We read the words of one that denied the judgement of the God of the Bible by denying the reality of sin and the need to confess such in His presence. We read the mind of one that has denied the necessity of the gospel to save from sin in favor of a system of working steps, a process salvation. These are not the same. The Big Book may help us in minor finite areas, but it cannot express to us eternal truths of the infallible God. As such, it cannot make us free.

The Big Book does not mesh with the Scriptures. Making any Scripture fit the Big Book, all the while denying the reality that the

## PART 1: THE POWER LACKING IN THE REMEDY OF THE WORLD

source of your addiction is sin and failing to conform to the God of the Scriptures, is to walk contrary to the light and truth of Christ. If God has given us "all things that pertain to life and godliness" in Christ, then that which denies Christ can offer us nothing but ungodly counsel, which threatens us with the end of the ungodly and not with the prosperous end of the righteous (Ps 1:5, 6). It misses the blessing of the truth of God. "Blessed is the man that walketh not in the counsel of the ungodly, nor standeth in the way of sinners, nor sitteth in the seat of the scornful. But his delight is in the law of the Lord; and in his law doth he meditate day and night. And he shall be like a tree planted by the rivers of water, that bringeth forth his fruit in his season; his leaf also shall not wither; and whatsoever he doeth shall prosper. The ungodly are not so: but are like the chaff which the wind driveth away" (Ps 1:1-4).

The Big Book claims to be a book of experience and offers that same experience to those who follow its text. As with all experience, we must ask of the experience if it is in line with the Scriptures. We must try the spirits to see if they are of God, because many false prophets are gone out into the world (1 John 4:1). When it comes to the declaration of a doctrine, which we declare with our mouths or through the conversation of our conduct, one is either a faithful witness or a false prophet. One is either declaring and offering that which corresponds to the Word of God, what God has declared, or they are declaring inventions of the mind and will of that which is not God. "Then the Lord said unto me, The prophets prophesy lies in my name: I sent them not, neither have I commanded them, neither spake unto them: they prophesy unto you a false vision and divination, and a thing of nought, and the deceit of their heart" (Jer 14:14). The warning in this matter of authority is clear, "See that ye refuse not him that speaketh. For if they escaped not who refused him that spake on earth, much more shall not we escape, if we turn away from him that speaketh from heaven . . . " (Heb 12:25).

Bill Wilson, the founder of the 12-steps, openly professed that the psychologist William James, known as the father of American psychology, was the direct influence of the development

## TRADEOFF # 4

of the steps. Reading after James, Wilson obtained the founding principles of AA highlighting the need of religious experience to conquer the disease of alcoholism. James prescribed the seeking of religious experience as a pragmatic means of changing behavior. This is known as the will to believe, much like the will to power of Fredrick Nietzsche (both precursors of existentialism and its denial of absolute truth, one says doing becomes truth and the other says believing becomes truth). It was taught that to change one's thinking empowered them to change their behavior. It is purely a humanistic ideology like the idea of the power of positive thinking that has gained religious tenants in the last few decades. This is still the basis of mental health models of treatment such as Cognitive Behavioral Therapy.

The religious experience described by James was to move one from calamity, to an admission of utter defeat, to an appeal to a belief in some higher power. This was mirrored by the foundational beliefs of Wilson to move the alcoholic from the inability to manage their own life, to admitting that there was no human help for them, to believing that a god could help. This is not a description of biblical repentance or the faith of Christ as some have claimed. It is not being confronted with the truth of God as a sinner and turning to God from that sin. This is simply becoming dissatisfied with the consequences of the sin one loves and building a system of belief to improve oneself. It did not matter if what one believed was true in the absolute sense. I have heard people in the program say things like, "would you rather be right or be happy." This is the residual effect of the belief of James, that a belief is true only if it proves to be useful to the one that believes it. Truth, therefore, is wholly subjective in the mind of the individual. As long as what one believes helps them to move from calamity to recovery, it is verifiable and cannot be questioned. As long as believing affects change, it does not matter if the substance of that belief is Satanism, Islam, Nazism, or a flying-spaghetti monster. All are now equally true by virtue of the effect they produced. This created a big tent for all beliefs to be applied to recovery. Faith in faith now replaces faith in the one true God. Belief in belief now replaces the need to believe upon the Christ of the Scriptures. One does not need to have evidence to support one's belief, as long as that belief was effective in their life.

On this basis, Bill Wilson sought and found a religious experience that worked for him. The Big Book offers that experience to its readers. The philosophy of James regarding religious truth was that experience produces truth and not truth experience. This is a direct contradiction of Christ who taught, "If ye continue in my word, then are ye my disciples indeed; And ye shall know the truth, and the truth shall make you free" (John 8:31, 32). Salvation begins with the word of Christ and our believing and following that faith. Doing so, the truth produces the experience of freedom.

For James, doctrine was the attempt to express experience. All doctrine is a weak attempt to describe the indescribable experience. Again, this coincides with atheistic existentialism. This may be captured best in the allegory of the ten blind men trying to describe their experience of touching the parts of an elephant. One held the tail and said it was a rope, one the belly and said it was a wall, and another the trunk and said it was a snake. The allegory ignores that there was a truth that existed, there was an elephant, and reduced all truth statements to vanity. Christ disagreed. James sought all manner of religious experience from necromancy, to séances, to pantheistic experiences. The adherents of the 12-steps follow that same mold. One can be spiritual without adhering to any form of doctrine. It is wholly about producing health. The religious experience moves one from being sick to being whole (see appendix for the biblical progress towards health). That fits well with a program that denies or ignores the actual existence of sin and guilt and the actual need for salvation. For the Christian, it is the form of the doctrine of the gospel that produces a true change in the heart (Rom 6:17).

The Big Book rejects the God of Abraham, the God of the Scriptures, in favor of a god that cannot truly be known. The God of the Scriptures, however, is Light. He has revealed Himself. The only begotten Son has declared Him (John 1:18). He has become partakers of our flesh (Heb 2:14). He has made Himself known.

## TRADEOFF # 4

There is truth and that truth is incarnate. The apostles handled that Word of Life (1 John 1:1-4). That is the difference between the Bible and the Big Book. The Bible declares the truth of God, and the Big Book leads men to choose their own god. The Bible declares Christ, of whom the volume of the book is written (Ps 40:7), but the Big Book gives you a god that has not been and cannot be revealed. The Bible is a record of the Most High making Himself known in space and time, the God that made a covenant with men. Ultimately, it presents us with the God that is Sovereign in the matter of redemption of sinful men. The Big Book offers us only a god that passively waits for us to do or decide to do. The Bible tells us of a God that promised the Messiah and sent His Son. It tells us of a God that seeks and draws man to salvation. It tells us of a God who raises us to new life from our dead condition of sin through the new birth. It tells us of a salvation that is all of God and not based on who we are, what we will do, or what our community wills on our behalf (John 1:12, 13). The Big Book offers only an undefinable religious experience based on the teachings of William James and not on the apostles and prophets of the one true God (Eph 2:18-22).

Here then is an equally devastating tragedy for those who believe they can seek God through the 12-steps. The 12-steps first reduce God to our own understanding. Then the steps tell us to make a decision to turn our will and our lives over to the care of that god that is limited to our own understanding, thus making our understanding alone our guide. To teach people to create their own god and then to tell them to do the will of that god is to leave them lost. It leaves us with no way or means, outside of our own understanding, to know the expressed will of God, to know what we are supposed to do. The steps leave four implied ways to know the will of God within its own framework. First, we could see the will of God as synonymous with our own understanding. Second, we can assume that the will of God is synonymous with the steps. Third, we could say that the will of God is synonymous with traditions of the community. Fourth, we can see the will of God as synonymous with the experience that is produced by the steps.

There is nothing that leads adherents to believe that there is an expressed and revealed will of God outside of those possibilities. Each of these is faulty and, even if combined, fail to give us any real understanding of what should be done. If you have a leaky bucket, it will not hold water. If you put four leaky buckets together, it will still not hold water. All of this is summed up in the warning that, "There is a way which seemeth right unto a man, but the end thereof are the ways of death" (Prov 14:12).

If we say that the will of God is synonymous with our understanding, then we choose to trust in our own understanding or rather to trust our own thinking. This is a direct violation of the Scriptures. "Trust in the Lord with all thine heart; and lean not unto thine own understanding" (Prov 3:5). The fool trusts in his own heart (Prov. 28:26). The heart of man is deceitful above all things (Jer 17:9). This is contrary to the clear declaration of the lost condition of man. "There is none righteous, no, not one: There is none that understandeth, there is none that seeketh after God. They are all gone out of the way, they are together become unprofitable; there is none that doeth good, no, not one" (Rom 3:10-12). Your understanding cannot get you to God and without Christ, you cannot discern the will of God. It is "Christ Jesus, who of God is made unto us wisdom, and righteousness, and sanctification, and redemption" (1 Cor 1:30).

If we say that the will of God is the steps that follow our decision to turn our will over to God, which is the natural assumption of the reading of the steps, then we rely on our works to atone or rather we trust our own will. We give ourselves over to the continual keeping of the steps. This becomes a blind leap into the realm of our own will to do, reminding us of the Jamesian will to believe or even the Nietzschean will to power. All of this is beyond any real revealed understanding of what is right and wrong behavior in the absolute sense. Whereas, we above deified our understanding. We here deify our will as the means of salvation. We say that doing the steps is equal to doing the will of God. Christ said that the work of God is to believe on the one that God sent (John 6:29). To say that the will of God is an arbitrary list of things for me to do, absent from Christ, is to live a life contrary to the Scriptures.

If we say that the traditions of the 12-step community are synonymous with the will of God, then we place the will of men at the same level as the expressed will of God or rather we trust in the traditions of men. In the 12 traditions of AA and NA, tradition number 2, it is expressly stated that the only authority is God who is expressed in the group conscience. We enter then into a system where the collective experiences of the continuing treatment community become greater than the commands of the Scriptures. The group becomes the final authority regarding what God is saying. We will talk more of this shortly. We give ourselves over to the authority of men and not God. The sponsor becomes the voice of God. The advice given at the meetings become expressions of God's will. "If we receive the witness of men, the witness of God is greater: for this is the witness of God which he hath testified of his Son. He that believeth on the Son of God hath the witness in himself: he that believeth not God hath made him a liar; because he believeth not the record that God gave of his Son" (1 John 5:9, 10). Christ has warned us against making the word of God of no effect by our traditions (Mark 7:13, Col 2:8).

If we say that the experience that is produced is synonymous with the will of God, then we make the ends the justifier of all things or rather we trust in the hope of the experience. There is no reason for us to believe that just because there is a desired result that it was the right means that produced it or that it was the will of God. To do the right thing, one must do the right thing by the right means for the right purpose. It may be God's will for us to be sober, no doubt it is, but it is not God's will to deny Him to become sober. It may be God's will for us to pay our bills, but it is not His will for us to rob a bank to do it. The existential experience is not the arbiter of absolute truth. Believe not every spirit (1 John 4:1).

The authority of our own understanding, our own will, the will of others, or the experience itself cannot tell us anything about the expressed will of God. The Bible itself contains the imperatives for our life that came from God revealed to us through

Christ. The Big Book only directs us into a circle of studying and working the steps in an endless cycle and perpetual mantra. Much of its advice is valuable, but it does not and cannot convey the will of God. You will never hear the need to search the Scriptures to find Christ in the rooms of AA and NA. The only way to break conformity to the world is through the renewing of your mind (Rom 12:1, 2). There is one from heaven that has spoken, and we should be careful not to reject Him. "See that ye refuse not him that speaketh. For if they escaped not who refused him that spake on earth, much more shall not we escape, if we turn away from him that speaketh from heaven" (Heb 12:25).

The imperative of God is clear, "This is my beloved Son, in whom I am well pleased; hear ye him" (Matt 17:5). To know the will of God, one must know Christ and hear His voice. Christ said, "My sheep hear my voice, and I know them, and they follow me" (John 10:27). The will of God is not some ineffable thing that is only discerned by one's emotions or a select group of enlightened people. It can be heard through the word of God. To know the will of God, one must know the Word of God and know how to apply it. To know the Word of God, one must follow Christ and Christ alone. We cannot choose a process of recovery over hearing the word of Christ. We must know Him and grow in the grace and knowledge of Him (2 Pet 3:18).

# Tradeoff # 5

NEXT, ONE MUST TRADE *the New Testament church for being in the rooms.* As we have already noted in passing, the idea that only an addict can understand and help another addict is wrong. Being an addict is not some special class of sin. All temptations that take men are common to men (1 Cor 10:13). The missing truth in the perception that people outside of addiction are unequipped to address addiction is that addiction to substances is sin; it is indicative of one's rebellion against God and the effects thereof. At the root of that rebellion is the unbelief of God and absence of the fear of God. Further, such a perception fails to understand the nature of the gospel and its power to remit sin and the power of the Word of God to speak to all areas of life. Once these truths are ascertained, there is help and understanding in the community of disciples. Sinners can understand other sinners. Saved sinners can help other saved sinners. They can administer grace to one another through Christ and His Word. They can bear one another's burdens. They can do what an addict or a group of addicts cannot do, speak to the real problem and the real solution. Once one identifies as a sinner, there is help for that one in Christ and His church. Once one is in the church, there is further help in their identity with Christ and the people of Christ. The church collectively is what each believer is individually. They are followers of Christ, followers of the one true Shepherd. "My sheep hear my voice, and I know them, and they follow me" (John 10:28). We have the privilege as a church to be a part of His flock with others that follow Him.

    The idea of church has fallen in our Western culture. Church is seen by most as a loose kind of club that one attends a couple times per year. The radical may even attend for a couple hours per week. However, there is no real sense of companionship with those there. It is just a religious exercise. People rely on themselves to meet their own needs or the ones they deem to be their family. When that fails, it does not even cross the mind of the individual that there is help in the church. Some, at their lowest, may view the church as a place to go for help with rent or food. Nevertheless, outside of the possibility of getting the church to help with material needs, the church is not seen as a place for emotional and spiritual help and health. It is a far cry from the sympathetic and compassionate interconnectedness that is described by Paul (Rom 12 & 1 Cor 12). The church meets the needs of the community. There is a need in all men to belong and find their identity in a community or group. If the church is not providing that need, the void will be filled by some other community. If that community is not after truth and the knowledge of the one true Shepherd, then that group will not minister to their true needs.

The 12-step meetings replace all the functions of the church as a spiritually supportive community. Church is fine, but meetings are the necessity for living a life free from addiction. However, this community has already denied the Most High and the problem of sin, replacing them with the authority of one's own understanding and the greater authority of the group conscience. It has replaced grace with a system of works. In the rooms of 12-step programs, they adopt the language of Christianity and call each other brothers and sisters. They do all of this in defiance of what they generally perceive to be a judgmental and unforgiving church that preaches the truth of God and the reality of sin. One does not have to study 12-step programs long to conclude that they borrow heavily from the model of the early New Testament church. Nevertheless, it does this without the necessity of a doctrinal commitment to any of the essential elements of the church or any essential connectedness to God and His Son.

One is often confronted with inevitable comparisons between the meeting and the church. The religious advocates of AA will talk about all the similarities to boast of the goodness of the meetings. Non-believers will use the AA model to rebuke the church for not being loving, caring, or accepting. The end result of both is to lift

## TRADEOFF # 5

up 12-step meetings as being on par or better than the church. This lessens the value of the church.

In fact, the traditions of the 12 steps speak of the unity of the group as necessary to salvation. The first of their 12 traditions, as laid out in the Big Book, teaches that the common welfare of the group should be first in the life of its members. There is no personal recovery without the unity of the group. It uses the language of Paul about the unity of the church. However, it explicitly teaches that salvation comes from the meetings by saying that the group must continue to live or death would result for many. The traditions not only teach that salvation is from the group but so is final authority. The second tradition blatantly says that there is only one ultimate authority, which is the god expressed in the group conscience. The traditions go on to encourage no outside affiliation for any group or member, which includes sectarian religious issues. It is not acceptable for members to affiliate with doctrines outside of the group conscience. Therefore, the group is the means of salvation and the final authority, and any system of belief outside of it is strongly discouraged. This is a distorted view of the church, which is neither a means of salvation or the final authority. This borrows from a model of the church that is more closely related to Roman Catholic ecclesiology, which teaches that salvation and final authority are found alone in the church. Nevertheless, people who enmesh themselves in treatment find themselves insulated from feeling any need to seek the people of God and follow Christ through the church. The 12-step group is all they believe they need. Like any cult or subculture, the program separates the individual from any message or belief outside of the group.

What do we lose? We lose that thing that is connected with Christ and truth. It is Christ that built the church. Christ said, "I will build my church; and the gates of hell shall not prevail against it" (Matt 16:18). Christ began the institution of the church. It is His body, that which is in His name doing His work in this world. AA meetings cannot make such a boast. They cannot, based on their structure, be Christ centered or claim to be His followers. Christ further declared in the context of the local New Testament church,

"Where two or three are gathered together in my name, there am I in the midst of them" (Matt 18:20). Being unable to meet in the name of Christ, the rooms of AA cannot offer any real connection to Christ or salvation (Acts 4:12). Losing connection to the church, they lose connection to that entity which is central to spiritual warfare and the only place of victory. There is no promise that the gates of Hell will not prevail against the treatment community, but there is such a promise of the institution of the church.

Being separated from Christ, there is a separation from the vital ministry of the church to minister the love of Christ to one another (2 John 4:7, 8). We give up on the very thing that will foster nourishment through the truth of God's Word. "He gave some, apostles; and some, prophets; and some, evangelists; and some, pastors and teachers; For the perfecting of the saints, for the work of the ministry, for the edifying of the body of Christ: Till we all come in the unity of the faith, and of the knowledge of the Son of God, unto a perfect man, unto the measure of the stature of the fullness of Christ . . . " (Eph 4:11-13). We trade the experience of the love of God that can be shared as a church. "Husbands, love your wives, even as Christ also loved the church, and gave himself for it . . . " (Eph 5:25). We lose a community that truly is concerned about keeping us from sin that separates us from Christ. And forsaking Christ, we forsake that which gives true unity and promotes true health; "From whom the whole body fitly joined together and compacted by that which every joint supplieth, according to the effectual working in the measure of every part, maketh increase of the body unto the edifying of itself in love" (Eph 4:16). Christ is "the Head, from which all the body by joints and bands having nourishment ministered, and knit together, increaseth with the increase of God" (Col 2:19). We will add shortly that, separate from the church, we are separated from true ministry and purpose (Matt 28:18-20).

So why would someone choose something less than the local church community for that which is loosely based upon it? Why trade our gold for lead? There are two chief complaints with the church. First, the church is claimed to be cold and uncaring.

## TRADEOFF # 5

Mostly, this complaint is levied by those who reject "hell fire and damnation" and all forms of what they call judgmentalism. Any organized body that says that sin exists and God is a God of judgement is dismissed. This is an entrenched position devoted to resisting the Most High and maintaining that their sin is not their fault. It is to continue to eat the poison, without care for the side effects. Admittedly, many churches fail to follow Christ and present His truth in love. For the sincere, there is no reason to give up on church. We should either work to make the church what it ought to be or find a church that is what it should be. However, if the motive for choosing the rooms of AA over the fellowship of a church is to avoid the judgement of sin and the worship of the Most High, then it speaks of one's lost condition. To such, I would beg them to be reconciled to God. Until then, the church cannot do them, any good and the best they can look forward to is a sober life now. In eternity, they will bow before the Most High and confess their sin before His judgement (Phil 2:10, Rev 20:11-16). However, it will be too late then.

The second reason for embracing meetings over the church is the therapeutic aspect. It defaults back to the pragmatic issue of my needs being met. The folly of what is called Christianity in America lends itself to this error. Church is not, in their minds, about worship of Christ or even ministering to the needs of those there. It is about meeting my own needs. Sermons are centered around ways to overcome hundreds of mental health hang ups and allowing people to leave feeling better about themselves, never having to leave sin to follow Christ (Matt 9:9). For people struggling with the hurt of their sin (i.e. consequences, emotional and social hang-ups, etc.), AA meetings can appear to meet their needs better than the church. It offers the bumper sticker answers to their surface issues that meet their immediate therapeutic needs.

There are two great errors regarding the role of the church in this thread. One is the belief that the church can only speak to a spiritual need and matters of addiction, as well as most mental health needs, are not spiritual. Therefore, if one needs help with addiction, which is a physical and biological problem, according to them, then it lies outside the realm of the church. One cannot simply dismiss the use and place of therapy and medication in some instances. However, if the system of therapy is directly opposed to the Scriptures, then we reject truth to trust in those things. God has given us all things pertaining to life and godliness (2 Pet 1:4). To believe that the ideas of Freud and James, and the systems they created, are just as valid and useful as the truth of the Scriptures is wrong headed and dangerous. It is the creation and setting up of a false idol one chooses to trust instead of the truth that is administered through the church.

 God does not speak equally through all sources and people. What was said by Jim Jones is not on par with the apostle Paul. Therefore, what is spoken through the traditions of the AA community is not equally true with that which was built on the foundation of the apostles and prophets. In the church, a true church, we have a community of people that are striving to be faithful witnesses together of the truths of God, striving to hear and know the voice and words of their one true Shepherd. If the rooms of AA are faithful to their traditions, traditions built on William James and ideas of creating one's own conception of God, then they are perpetuating ideas opposed to the truth. There is nothing therapeutic about eating rat poison, regardless of the amount of good food it contains. The mantra that all truth is God's truth is meant to instill the idea that all sources of truth are equal. This is false. God is the God of truth. He alone is just and right (Deut 32:4). Any community or system that speaks falsely of Him or contradicts what He has clearly revealed is a lie. A half-truth is a whole lie. I heard one advocate for the 12-steps say that they believed Christ to be the source of all salvation, but that there were many paths to get there. They went on to say that, in the spirit of the 12-steps, to believe otherwise is to believe that one is saved by believing on a set of certain doctrines and not by Christ. While this sounds pious, it ignores the idea that there is a God that has spoken. The true church says to hear Him and believe His words, which is the only means of knowing Him.

## TRADEOFF # 5

The second error is the belief that the church should be geared toward a therapeutic self-discovery and self-help strategies. Many churches have embraced the idea that church is all about self-improvement, making us good people who function in harmony with the lost world. As such, the job of the church is to promote self-improvement and help the people to build better positive self-images. They see the church as ministering to Maslow's hierarchy of needs, the goal of which is the self-actualization of each individual. The good side of this focus is the realization among ministry workers that, at the base level, meeting the needs of the hungry and suffering around us is important. The side effect is that the pews become full of people who believe that the chief end of church is for them to have their needs met. If the music does not entertain, if the message does not stir them or validate them, if there are not sufficient activities for them and their family, then their needs are not being met. The church community is not supposed to be like that or seen as meeting that function. It is a place of worship to the Most High, through Christ the only way to the Most High. It is where we humble ourselves and rejoice together in the mercy and truth of that one true God and minister His truth and love to one another. For a church to be something less than that, is for a church to fail to promote the health and help of its members.

The rooms of AA cannot perform the vital function of a worshipping and ministering community. People will attend the meetings with the same desire for their needs to be met. Sadly, they will find something that on the surface appears more honest and more healing. They will leave the meeting more encouraged than when they came. They speak "their truth" and listen to others do the same. They feel connected now. However, they have failed to worship the one true God with their community. They failed to rest in Christ in the rooms. They failed to minister "the truth" and "the love" to anyone around them. In so doing, they failed to get the true health and help of God (See appendix).

There is a pervasive love of self that is demonstrated in the rooms of AA and NA. Love of self is highly promoted in the ideology. One advocate once told me that Jesus taught the need for

## PART 1: THE POWER LACKING IN THE REMEDY OF THE WORLD

a love for self, which they said forms the basis for loving others. This is a misunderstanding of the second great commandment to love your neighbor as yourself. That does not mean that we must learn to love ourselves, but that all men naturally do. The law calls them to limit that self-love to meet the needs of their neighbor. Where the love of self is, there is a lack of love for others and there is an absence of a love or desire after the true and living God. As stated already, prayer is reduced to a desire for God to serve our needs. The Serenity Prayer is not a collective submission to the will of God, but a collective request for self-serving knowledge and personal peace. The process of public confession is also self-serving and directly contrary to the Scriptures. The average meeting is marked by public confessionals of the vile thoughts of select members as they describe their struggles with desiring their sinful compulsions. They delight in the fact that they can go there and unload their sinful thoughts, which would, according to their own minds, be judged if spoken in the church. The way of the fool is the despising of wisdom in favor of uttering and discovering the thoughts of their own heart (Prov 18:2). There they need to not let go of any sinful desire. The only necessity is for them to state a desire to stop their addiction.

After that, they are there unfettered, free to do as they please as long as the desire not to actualize the desire to use substances to which they are addicted. The average group will excuse all manner of sexual immorality among its adherents. The unspoken thirteenth step, for many, is to find someone at the meeting to engage in sexual immorality, though they "should" wait one year to work on the steps first. The group is what allows for all forms of evil to remain in one's life, outside of a desire to stop the addiction. The collective conscience has no ability to speak in a real way on anything as wrong. It must even say continued substance abuse is acceptable, for relapse is part of treatment. It speaks not with the voice of Christ to go and sin no more (John 8:11). It can never say that something is not the will of God to do. The love of self leads one to be a lover of pleasure more than of God (1 Tim 3:4). It further reveals a love of darkness instead of light. The meeting is just

## TRADEOFF # 5

salve for the conscience, a fix differing little from the life of addiction for the one that says, "I just really need a meeting right now."

This is not to speak evil of all that these groups do. One may find encouragement in these groups toward a nominal good. One may even find a group heavily influenced by Christian doctrine. It is the structure of the steps and traditions that cause it to fail to measure up to the reality of the church. The steps and traditions limit the speaking of the absolute truth of the gospel, the reality of sin, and the worship of the one true God. As such, there can be no fellowship with Christ who is in the midst of them that come together in His name (Matt 18:20). As such, there can be no true worship of the Father who seeks true worshippers to worship in spirit and truth (John 4:23). There can be no true conviction of the Holy Spirit who is the Spirit of truth and testifies of Christ (John 15:26). There is therefore no fellowship with or worship of God. It is a congregation that denies God, sin, and the truth of God even at its best. It may be acceptable for a lost person to be yoked with such groups, though they insulate them from understanding the truths of the Gospel, but it would never be acceptable for a believer to be unequally yoked with unbelievers (2 Cor 6:14). The Christian loves and seeks to support those that are born of God (1 John 3). "Lord, I have loved the habitation of thy house, and the place where thine honor dwelleth. Gather not my soul with sinners . . . " (Ps 26:8, 9). There is no good that can come from gathering with a group that cannot honor the one true God.

# Tradeoff # 6

ONE FINAL TRADEOFF IS *perpetuating the 12-steps instead of preaching the gospel of Christ.* The steps and traditions speak of giving back as the singular purpose after producing a spiritual awakening through the steps. One must have a purpose moving forward and this is the expressed meaning of life according to the steps and traditions. One must give back to the steps. One must care singularly about the addict still in active addiction and take the steps to them now. If not, the steps will quit working for them. The traditions speak of the steps now as a message to be carried to the alcoholic or addict that still suffers. The language is directly borrowed from the Christian mandate found in the Great Commission of Christ to preach His gospel to every creature. Thus, the treatment sets itself as an alternative gospel to be carried to sinners and gives the addict an alternate purpose of doing something less than the commission of Christ.

The spiritual and religious nature of 12-step treatments are inherent. Nevertheless, this is where the steps leave status of treatment to the status of an organized religion. The steps and traditions in the end demand proselytizing. Unlike treatments in the medical and mental health fields, the steps give people a message to carry. They have good news or a gospel to take to addicts who are suffering. They go about saying that their lives are saved by the keeping of these steps; and if one will do the same, they can live too. The integration of evangelization as a part treatment confronts the committed Christian with the truth that this is indeed another gospel, directly opposed to the gospel of Christ.

Make no mistake, this is not asking the participant of the treatment to be enthusiastic about a product. This is a lifelong commitment to the evangelism of the message of the steps to a world of people that are said to die without it. It defines a purpose

## TRADEOFF # 6

of missionary life that is necessary to the maintenance of one's own salvation or sobriety, thus betraying the essential works-based salvation theology inherent in the steps that are opposed to the grace of the gospel. It is a lifelong commitment to support the group. It is the real point where the participant is to give themselves over to live the life of the steps and preach it to others.

This would not be a point of contention if that life and doctrine that they were giving themselves over to, to live and declare, was true. If one were healed of his cancer by the use of a particular treatment, then it would stand to reason that they would enthusiastically tell all that suffer from cancer that they need that treatment. However, as we have seen, it calls one to worship something less than the Most High God. It denies the reality of sin that separates people from God. It leads people to trust in keeping the steps instead of believing the gospel. It declared the authority of individual and collective conscience over the authority of what God has revealed in His Word. To preach such a message is to make oneself an enemy of the gospel of Christ. It does not heal anyone; it traps them in an endless process of salvation. It keeps them from knowing the truths that could heal. To perpetuate such a gospel is to carry a curse to others, to give poison to those who need healing (Gal 1:6-9).

The gospel is different. The gospel is God-given, God-wrought, and God-empowered. It is the truth. It is pure. Any other message is tainted and lacks the authority of God. It lacks the demonstrated power that is connected to the resurrection of Christ (Rom 1:4), which is what can empower the individual to walk in newness of life (Rom 6:5, 6). It is a message that lacks the convicting power of the Holy Spirit (John 14, 15, & 16). You "shall receive power, after that the Holy Ghost is come upon you: and ye shall be witnesses unto me . . . " (Acts 1:8). When one carries the 12-step gospel, they have only the authority of men, but the witness of God is greater (1 John 5:9). When one carries a false gospel they carry only the subjective power of personal experience, but the true gospel is the objective reality that Christ is the truth (John 14:6). When one carries the 12-step gospel, they carry a message of moral ambiguity and salvation only from circumstances in life, but the gospel carries the witness and conviction of sin and righteousness and draws men to eternal life. The preaching of the gospel of Christ is the witness of the truth. The truth alone makes men free. The gospel alone is the power of God unto salvation (Rom 1:16). What greater purpose is there for any person than to declare the good news of Christ (how His death, burial, and resurrection on behalf of the condemned sinner saves men from the wrath of the holy God and how whoever received Him as Lord and Savior is made righteous). What a tragedy to give your life to declaring something less.

# Part 2: The Power of the Gospel over Addiction

LEAVING BEHIND THE WORLDLY remedies for sobriety, consider the power of the gospel. The offer of the gospel speaks of the greatest need of man, salvation from sin, and life from the dead. To stop at sobriety and not address the matter of sin, as we have seen, is to fail to address the real need. Each person is alienated from God due to their sin. Separated from the life that is in God, we face eternal death. The gospel is that which reconciles us to the holy and just God. Christ alone brings us to God. Christ then causes us to walk in newness of life. The power of the gospel is the power to change men. Christ changed Lazarus by His Word. The same power was displayed by Christ when He said to Matthew, "follow me," and Matthew left all and followed Him. This power is what we offer. The power of a new life is what is needed.

We do not need to again lay the foundation of sobriety or freedom from sin by examining the truths, lacking in the world's answers to addiction. There is a Most High God that we should seek and who alone defines Himself. There is moral truth and we are guilty sinners before that holy and just God. There is a gospel that alone can save without the works of our flesh that can by no means make us right with God. There is only one final and authoritative voice to be believed and that is the Word of God who is light without darkness. There are true people of God who have believed the absolute truth of God's word. They are not perfect; but as saved sinners, they alone can be ministers to the needs of other sinners who come to Christ. There is only one gospel to be preached to the world and that is the good news of Christ, which alone can meet the true needs of all that hear it. Building on that we consider the deeper truths that can transform the sinner (the addict) into a follower or disciple of Christ. Let us consider some necessary truths of this changed life.

# Necessity # 1

FIRST, THE UNDERLYING COMPONENT of a changed life is *the fear of God*. "By mercy and truth iniquity is purged: and by the fear of the Lord men depart from evil" (Prov. 16:6). These words confront us with the reality of a holy God and how He relates to our daily behavior before Him. Solomon said elsewhere, "A wise man feareth, and departeth from evil: but the fool rageth, and is confident" (Prov 14:16). Men will sin by ignoring the reality of God. Contrariwise, when people fear God the natural result is they stop their sin. This is wisdom. "Be not wise in thine own eyes: fear the Lord, and depart from evil" (Prov 3:7). The opposite truth is that, where no fear of God is attained, men are emboldened in an evil way. It is "The transgression of the wicked" that plainly teaches us "that there is no fear of God before his eyes" (Ps 36:1). They act in wickedness believing in their heart that there will be no reckoning. The fear of the Lord is to hate evil and the absence of that fear is to love it (Prov 8:13). Modern Bible teachers have foolishly and falsely taught that the Christian or anyone else should not fear God. They take texts out of context regarding perfect love casting out fear (1 John 4:18, which speaks of the security of the believer in the love of God from the fear of God turning them away) or God not giving us the spirit of fear (2 Tim 1:7, which speaks of our boldness in Christ before sinful men) to teach against necessary fear. It is fearful to fall into the hands of the living God (Heb. 10:31). Christ taught us to fear (Matt 10:28). Christians are to walk in fear (Acts 9:31, Eph 5:21, Col 3:22). We can, as a matter of clear New Testament teaching, only perfect holiness in the fear of God (2 Cor 7:1).

    There is a type of fear toward God that is not right. The Scriptures speak of godly fear (Heb 12:28), which implies that there is a type of fear toward God that is ungodly. It is the ungodly fear that is often rebuked by God in His people when He says to "Fear not." Most of the time God speaks those words to men, it is to direct them not to fear something outside of God. Other times it is spoken to turn men from an ungodly fear of God. Adam said he hid from God because he was afraid (Gen 3:10). Israel said that they did not want to hear God speak because they were afraid (Exod 20:19, 20). The wicked servant said he buried the talent given to him by the Lord because he was afraid (Matt 25:25). When it speaks of the fearful being cast into the Lake of fire that speaks of those who fear contrary to faith (Rev 21:8). There is a slavish fear of religious works that says one cannot simply trust God to save by grace alone, but one must add a system of works. These are all examples of ungodly fear of God; fear that hides from God, will not hear God, will not trust God, and will not come before His presence. Such fear is discouraged by those who are received of God (Gen 15:1). Godly fear is to know God as true and holy and in faith to come to Him with joy and trembling (Ps 2:11). Godly fear is given to us of God in the new covenant and new birth. It makes us to not want to depart from Him, for there is only terror to infinite degrees outside of His presence (Jer 32:40). God should always be seen by us to be so great that we tremble at the sense of His presence, even with joy and faith and love knowing that He has accepted us in Christ. "Who is like unto thee, O Lord, among the gods? who is like thee, glorious in holiness, fearful in praises, doing wonders" (Exod 15:11)?

Much could be said about ungodly fear, but we need yet to fear in a godly way. The idea that God ought to be feared is foreign to Western forms of Christianity. Our churches have developed a tamed or domesticated view of God. They have defined God in such a way to highlight His love, but they have forgotten that He is holy and His love is a holy love. They have painted a picture of God desperately pleading with people to accept Him and have forgotten that He is omnipotent. They have developed traditions of God resembling more of a genie granting wishes to people who say the magic words or use the right formula and have forgotten that He is the final judge of all and all His ways are judgement

(Deut 32:4). They have created a God that saves all eventually forgetting that He has said that He hates the workers of iniquity and is known of us first in our conscience as a God of wrath (Ps 5:5, Rom 1:18). We are even told that the idea that we should fear God is not an enlightened view. God, they say, has made us the way we are and accepts us the way that we are because He is love. They imagine the nature of God to be as pliable as their sense of morality and imagine God to be the author of all their sin, which word they refuse to allow from their pulpits. They heap to themselves teachers to scratch their ears and meet their felt needs. Sunday mornings are there for God to serve us, to meet our therapeutic needs by telling us how good we are, how worthy we are, and how God is going to speak blessings into our lives. All the while, we willfully live lives contrary to what He has revealed His will to be. Church is about us learning ways to use God to help with our anxieties and depressive states.

We have declawed the lion and defanged the cobra, and we think we can do the same thing with God. However, God cannot be defined by us. God, in His nature, is greater than all. To make Him something less is dangerous. The idea of a domesticated God is foolish. We cannot tame creation as a whole or in part, why would we believe we could tame the one that, in unlimited power, made every creature. If a spider crawled on the legs of some, they would shrink in panic. A snake would have that effect on me. Yet, they are but creatures. If chased by a bear, we would run. If faced with a tsunami, we would wail. If stared down by the fiercest carnivore imagined, fear would seize us. However, the Creator we believe is not to be feared.

The wicked honestly believe they can rebel against God. They do this by lying to themselves about the nature of the God that is truly there. They do not want to retain God in their knowledge and God is not in all their thoughts. They drive Him from their thoughts and believe foolishly, like a child playing peek-a-boo, that God is no longer there (Ps. 10:4). They tell themselves that nothing bad will ever happen to them (Ps. 10:6). "Because sentence against an evil work is not executed speedily, therefore the heart of the sons of men is fully set in them to do evil" (Eccl 8:11). The wicked tell themselves that God does not see them and will not remember their deeds (Ps 10:11). They convince themselves that God will not avenge or do justice (Ps 10:13). God does know us. God does see us. God is writing a book of remembrance. God will open the books one day all will be naked before Him. He has commanded us to repent. He has warned of His judgement. He is Holy and pure and hates our sin. All the creatures we fear are indifferent to us. God is not indifferent to us. The unjust judge was unjust because he did not fear God. He did not believe God saw, knew him, or that he would answer to God for his injustice (Luke 18:2).

We cannot stand in the presence of holy omniscience, holy omnipotence, holy love, and divine goodness and not tremble at how unholy we are, how unlike God we are, how impure our thoughts, and how helpless we are before Him. When we see ourselves as we truly are before God, we cry out for the stains of our sins. Peter saw the holy God and said, "Depart from me for I am a sinful man." Isaiah saw the holiness of God and cried out, "Woe is me! for I am undone; because I am a man of unclean lips, and I dwell in the midst of a people of unclean lips: for mine eyes have seen the King, the LORD of hosts" (Isa 6:5). It causes us to see our spots and want them purged from us. We need the mercy of God. We need the truth of God.

When the Scriptures say, "By mercy and truth iniquity is purged . . . ," the term mercy and truth are synonymous with the fear of God described in the second part of the verse. It describes the nature of God that both terrifies and saves. It is God's mercy and not ours that can clear us who bear the reality of our iniquity. It is the truth of God that opens the wound bare and the mercy of God that cleanses us. We stand before a God that alone can show us mercy through the truth of His Word. He alone in His truth can see the true evil inside us. We pray in our fear that He will look upon us and know us, try us, and see the wickedness (Ps 139:23, 24). Those who fear not God will not desire Him to see them in truth. As such, they will keep their sins hidden and go on in darkness. When we are opened before God, we can seek mercy.

## NECESSITY # 1

Nevertheless, that fearful truth of who we are leaves us standing purely at His mercy. He does not have to save us or forgive us. He can cast us to the lowest Hell in His truth and it would be just. The trembling sinner cries out, "God, be merciful to me a sinner" knowing that God may freely have mercy on whom He pleases (Rom 9:15). There is no other way for a sinner to approach God. In addition, there is no other way for them to go home justified (Luke 18:13, 14). This is contrary to the modern evangelical hoops that are presented by churches, whereby we prescribe a list of steps and tell people that if they do this and that God must save them. We must approach God with the fear and reverence that His holy and awesome nature demands. "But there is forgiveness with thee, that thou mayest be feared" (Ps 130:4). No proud man approaching God without fear will ever know the forgiveness of Christ and the purging of their sins.

The same is true of their ability to live a life of holiness. They depart from evil in their walk by the same sense of fear. We are not to let that sense of the mercy and truth of God forsake us, we are to bind them to our daily lives (Prov 3:3). The fear of the Lord alone gives us the knowledge, understanding, and wisdom we need to live our lives (Prov 1:7, 9:10). We need the knowledge of the holy God. We need to see God and know God in His glory if we want to depart from sin. There is very little desire among professing Christians to know God. They do not seek Him in their work and they do not make Him the end of their pursuits. They perish for a lack of knowledge (Hos 4:6). This is the fountain of life by which we escape the snares of death (Prov 14:27).

When it comes to the matter of our substance use or addiction, we must allow the truth of God to diagnose it. It is evil. It is iniquity. God hates this sin, and I cannot do that which the Lord hates. We must see His sovereign hatred of our sin and we need not go any further than the cross of Christ to see that hatred of our sin displayed. We must come to God for mercy because of this evil in our lives. We must fall before Him praying for His mercy on the basis of the truth that He has revealed Himself to be a merciful God and has made a way for His mercy through that same cross.

Trembling before Him as sinners, we may come to know forgiveness of sins through Christ. In that same fear, we go forward away from evil. We perfect our holiness in the fear of God (2 Cor 7:1). We must live a life knowing that God knows and God sees. One lesson God taught Job was that he was nothing before the great creatures God has created. If Job could not contend with the behemoth or the leviathan, how could he contend with God (Job 40 & 41)? We cannot live lives before a holy God in brazen sin. We would not tempt the cobra to strike us or the shark to bite us. How foolish to tempt God with our sin. Fear Him that can destroy both body and soul in hell (Matt 10:28). "Serve the Lord with fear, and rejoice with trembling. Kiss the Son, lest he be angry, and ye perish from the way, when his wrath is kindled but a little. Blessed are all they that put their trust in him" (Ps 2:11, 12).

# Necessity # 2

Knowing, and by consequence, fearing God is foundational to being free from sin. We need to also *know ourselves* as we truly are before God. We need to know ourselves as sinners and know how exceedingly sinful our sin is in the eyes of our holy God (Rom 7:13). We must abandon all trust in ourselves and come humbly before God (Ps 118:8). We cannot trust ourselves or our own hearts. Our heart is "deceitful above all things, and desperately wicked: who can know it" (Jer 17:9)? There is an alienation that exists from our very self that came with the advent of sin (into humanity in Adam and in our personal experience by virtue of our sinful choices). We want that which is wrong. We desire darkness because our deeds are evil, and we are tormented with any light of goodness that shines (John 3:19-21). We do not understand our very hearts and the way we take; we only know that it is what we want, all the while hating our way and ourselves for taking it. The answer that Jeremiah gave to the question of who can know their own heart is, "I the Lord search the heart, I try the reins, even to give every man according to his ways, and according to the fruit of his doings" (Jer 17:10). We must then do the scary thing of stepping out into the light of God's truth and letting Him see us and judge us. "Search me, O God, and know my heart: try me, and know my thoughts: And see if there be any wicked way in me, and lead me in the way everlasting" (Ps 139:23, 24). This is how we move forward in the fear of the Lord, desiring God to see us, define us, and show us what we really are.

    We must get out of the mindset that we define ourselves. There is a tendency in us all to justify what we do and work to make ourselves look good. Just as we do not have the right to define God, so we do not have the right to define ourselves or our reality. We are not gods, but men. We do not make our own truth or reality. This is the fruit of pride just like the doctrine that we choose our own conception of God. We are presented with a reality not of our own choosing and limits that are not set by us. Try as we may, our limits are obvious. We cannot choose anything outside of our nature or circumstances. We cannot define gravity for ourselves and expect it to behave according to our will. We cannot bend numbers to fit what we want our budget to be. That does not mean that we run into the shelter of a fatalism or determinism, even if we paint it with divine colors. When we consider our deeds, the things we do and the things we desire, they were not things formed in us by God. God is not the author of our sin. We can never say that which is contrary to the revealed nature of God that God hath made me thus. "God hath made man upright; but they have sought out many inventions" (Eccl 7:29). This is the experience of all humanity. We all had a semblance of innocence that we tarnished by our own will (Rom 7:9). We all filled up the measure of original sin by seeking the fruit of our own way, our own imaginations and desires and inventions (Prov 1:31, Isa 53:6). You sought and desired those things contrary to God (Rom 1:18-32, Jas 1:13-15). God made you with a will, but you used that will to choose that which was not after God. For example, God made men sexual beings but did not cause them to rape, molest, commit adultery, or engage in any other sexual behavior. To define ourselves in such a way that is contrary to God's Word and then to defend it as being of God is the greatest example of a wicked heart. To stand up and say I am an alcoholic by nature is no different. We are sinners by our own choice. When we seek what God has forbade, we join the number of those who choose to rebel against the Most High. When we plunge the needle in our veins, breathe the fumes of our idol, or drown ourselves in spirits, we become ones who actively spit in the face of a holy and omnipotent God.

The problem lies in us, and it is this on which we want the Word of God to shed its light. To go on in that which is opposed to God and say we are of God is to live a lie (1 John 1:4-7). Once God has shown us the truth of ourselves and our works, we must make a choice between that thing and the fearful God. That drug is wrong. We know it is wrong because it has enticed us, it has moved itself aright, or rather in an alluring way, to go into darkness and away from light (Prov 23:29-35, Jas 1:14 - note, this answers the question of when alcohol becomes a sin, are we allured by it or enticed to give ourselves over to it?). If we must choose between our will and God's, we are morally responsible to choose God. If we refuse to choose God, we only prove ourselves as worthy candidates for His wrath. "If thine eye offend thee, pluck it out: it is better for thee to enter into the kingdom of God with one eye, than having two eyes to be cast into hell fire: Where their worm dieth not, and the fire is not quenched" (Mark 9:43-49). We need, in the light of what God has shown us and in the fear of God, to cut off and cast away anything that He shows us is contrary to Him. This is what is called repentance; and except ye repent, ye shall perish (Luke 13:3, 5).

We have a problem and the problem is not anything else but our own self. We think people judging our works are wrong. We get mad and say they cannot judge a book by its cover. We deny that those works came from that which is within us (Matt 15:17-20). Every faculty we have is given over to sin and that which opposes God. We are totally lost without Christ (Eph 2:12). We have that within us called the imagination. This speaks of the intelligence and planning of the mind of man. It is the place where the images and idols we bow down to are made (Rom 1:21-23). It has become that which is centered on evil continually and has been since our youth up (Gen 6:5, 8:21). The Lord sees these imaginations of ours (1 Chr 28:9). It is among those things that stink in His nostrils as abominations to Him (Prov 6:16-19). It is this thing in us that needs to be conquered by Christ (2 Cor 10:5). We have a depraved thought life that is separated from God. We have a thinking problem. No one knows this truth as intuitively as the addict does. Their thoughts and planning become centered on the activity of seeking, possessing, using, and enjoying that thing which most pleases themselves, regardless of the obvious moral hurdles they must ignore in doing so. The non-addict has the same problem. None of us would want our thoughts truly known by those around us. We steal, kill, maim, hurt, cheat, and all manner of ungodly things all within the confines of our own thoughts. There we define what our life is all about. These things need to be brought into the light of God.

Then there are our affections. What is it that we love? What is that thing that we are devoted to? The greatest of all commands is to love God with all. The second great command is to love our neighbors as ourselves. What we love will be seen in the things we do. We show in our deeds that we love only ourselves, the most base and natural form of love that exists. The addict robs their families to get their drug. They will lash out violently to loved ones who stand in the way of them and their high. In this, we show ourselves unworthy of God. You cannot serve or love two gods (Luke 16:13). With each act of devotion to our own pleasures, we spit at the one true God with disdain. "If any man love not the Lord Jesus Christ, let him be Anathema Maranatha" (1 Cor 16:22).

Our intellect and sensibilities being corrupt, so is our will or volition. Again, it is our own lust that causes us to commit sin (Jas 1:13-15). We find ourselves in the bondage of sinful addiction because we have freely and sinfully chosen to give ourselves over to them. We yielded to those things. We gave them right and control. "Know ye not, that to whom ye yield yourselves servants to obey, his servants ye are to whom ye obey; whether of sin unto death, or of obedience unto righteousness" (Rom 6:16)? You put yourself on the path of destruction. You gave it the right to command your obedience. The whole of the addiction is a testament to one's will, not to one's lack of will, and a testament that you have a will opposed to obedience toward God. "Then shall they eat of the fruit of their own way, and be filled with their own devices" (Prov 1:31).

One may object and say that the addict does not want to remain in the clutches of this taskmaster. They are indeed sad and broken. They shed tears over the things they do. They are miserable and depressed. Here, we see the tragedy of the victim, without setting aside the reality of their role as violators. They do weep. However, for what reason are they weeping? Sadly, too many weep like Esau. Esau wept over his inability to have the blessing and not over the birthright that he sold to satisfy his own flesh (Heb 12:16, 17). The addict too often weeps over their inability to have their lusts without the consequences. If they could have their drug without hurting their family then they would. Judas was sorrowful and even hated the silver he gained by betraying Christ. Just because sorrow exists does not mean that true repentance is present. That is what is needed, true repentance. A false repentance produces no change and ends in death. There is a godly sorrow that brings true repentance that brings true change. "Godly sorrow worketh repentance to salvation not to be repented of: but the sorrow of the world worketh death. For behold this selfsame thing, that ye sorrowed after a godly sort, what carefulness it wrought in you, yea, what clearing of yourselves, yea, what indignation, yea, what fear, yea, what vehement desire, yea, what zeal, yea, what revenge! In all things ye have approved yourselves to be clear in this matter" (2 Cor 7:10, 11). To weep over not getting to fully enjoy the sin you love is not godly sorrow that works repentance. It is further proof of the wickedness of one's heart. To hate that sin in the presence of a fearful, terrible, and holy God is the beginning of real repentance. The latter desires to be right with God. The former still desires to spit in the face of God if given a more convenient opportunity. It is important to see ourselves as we truly are, guilty before a holy God.

# Necessity # 3

THAT BRINGS US TO the need of *following Christ*, the Word of God, who alone can bring us to God. To understand the necessity of Christ, it is important first to understand the importance of the role of revelation in our life. God is a God to be feared. Our sinfulness is a truth about ourselves that we all intuitively know. We know in ourselves that God is a God of wrath against our sin, our conscience bearing witness. What we do not know is what God demands of us or rather how we can be right with God. Consider, therefore, that God has made Himself known. He is there, as Francis Schaefer has said, and He is not silent. We have the privilege of hearing and reading the Word of God. In that Word, we learn of the nature of our God in His glory confirming the truth of our fears. We learn of the truth of our condition before Him. We learn of His mercy and of the possibility of us knowing His mercy.

The Word of God will have one of two effects as it teaches us of God and reproves us. The fool will despise wisdom and instruction but those that fear God will find in it wisdom and knowledge (Prov 1:7). The one that wants their sin, the sinner, will recoil from its light and not allow it to correct them (John 3:19-21). The one that truly fears will come into its light and find its words a joy. The Word of God is a perfect mirror to show us, in the true light of God, our flaws. The fool will behold themselves in the mirror and walk away forgetting what they saw, never correcting their lives. The wise will behold themselves and continue in the truths that they see, having those flaws corrected thereby (Jas 1:21-25).

How does this relate to keeping us from sin or from the motions of sin, which are present in the state of addiction? The chief importance is its creative power. God spoke and all things came into existence. "By the word of the Lord were the heavens made; and all the host of them by the breath of his mouth" (Ps 33:6).

## NECESSITY # 3

He said let there be light and there was light. That same creative power is able to bring life from the dead. The word of Christ alone brought Lazarus from the grave and the time will come that all that are in the grave shall hear His voice (John 5:28). The power of the Word of God is something we can know and experience by faith. When we trust in the gospel, or the faith of Christ, we come to know the truth of salvation. We become new creations of God, newly born into new life (2 Cor 5:17, John 3:3, 5, 7, 16). This is the through the power of the Word and Words of God, "Being born again, not of corruptible seed, but of incorruptible, by the word of God, which liveth and abideth for ever" (1 Pet 1:23). It is the engrafted Word of God; the Word of God joined to us by the full trust of our hearts and minds, that is able to save our souls (Jas 1:21). It has the power to give us life from our spiritual death and separation from God (Eph 2:1). Consider that the entrance of the Words of God into our lives gives light (Ps 119:30). Our salvation comes through believing God and that faith comes alone from the Word of God being heard by us (Rom 10:8-17). This experience of power takes us from being drunkards to being sanctified and justified before God. The Word of God is what bridges the fearful reality of a God that is holy and the truth of His holy love expressed in the gospel of Christ, where God provided by Himself salvation from His just wrath.

It is important for us to realize that the Word of God is not simply words to be obeyed. When we receive the Words of God in salvation, we become disciples or followers of Christ. That truth changes everything about how we live from this point. That does involve obedience. However, when we understand and know the miraculous power in the Word of God through salvation, we do not just obey but we love to obey. The Words of God and Christ become vehicles through which we show our worship, love, and devotion to our Lord who saved us. If we love Him, we keep His commands (John 14:15). We do not just do the words, we delight now to do them (Ps 40:8). It makes sense to us now to know that the longest chapter in the Bible is written about love for the Word of God (Ps 119).

## PART 2: THE POWER OF THE GOSPEL OVER ADDICTION

This life of discipleship and love is what leads us away from our sinfulness. "Wherewithal shall a young man cleanse his way? by taking heed thereto according to thy word. With my whole heart have I sought thee: O let me not wander from thy commandments. Thy word have I hid in mine heart, that I might not sin against thee" (Ps 119:9-11). The treatment community still has not divorced themselves from the language of cleansing in relationship to dealing with their addiction. They speak of getting clean and staying clean from drugs or alcohol. The language betrays a greater need than most of them realize. When they speak of being clean, they speak, most usually, of stopping that which is wrong in their life. They believe that if they can simply stop sinning and keep themselves from sinning in that same way any further that they will be clean. They make the mistake of believing that the outward cleansing equals the inward cleansing as well, a mistake prevalent in all religions. Christ warned, "cleanse first that which is within the cup and platter, that the outside of them may be clean also" (Matt 23:26). When the Christian speaks of cleansing, they speak of the total cleansing from all sin through the gospel of Christ. They speak of a conscience purged from evil beneath the forgiveness of Christ. All cleansing comes only from the blood of our substitute who died in our place. The book of Leviticus speaks more on the matter or cleansing than any other book, and it is always on the basis of shed blood of a sacrifice. "And almost all things are by the law purged with blood; and without shedding of blood is no remission" (Heb 9:22). Only God can bring the clean out of the unclean (Job 14:4).

The question before us now then is this, "How then can man be justified with God? or how can he be clean that is born of a woman" (Job 25:4)? This the psalmist tells us comes only from the Word of God, by us taking heed to it. We find ourselves bound in the leprosy of sin, unclean, outside of grace. The Word of God tells us that Jesus passes by and, if He wills, He can make us clean (Matt 8:2, 3). We can hear His pronouncement, "Now ye are clean through the word which I have spoken unto you" (John 15:2). The Word of God comes and tells us to turn to Christ, and we obey

## NECESSITY # 3

the gospel by believing upon Him and repent toward Him away from our sinful condition. By taking heed and responding to the preaching of the gospel, we are made clean.

Being made clean, we can also be kept clean by the Word. We can walk in the light of His fellowship and find fresh cleansing. "But if we walk in the light, as he is in the light, we have fellowship one with another, and the blood of Jesus Christ his Son cleanseth us from all sin . . . . If we confess our sins, he is faithful and just to forgive us our sins, and to cleanse us from all unrighteousness" (1 John 1:7, 9). We can walk with Christ, learn of Christ, and joyously have Him cleanse us from all that is contrary to Him. This is a joyous work of love Christ has taken up (Eph 5:26). This gets into a greater aspect of our cleansing. We have been bonded to Christ. We are now one with Him. We are in Him, as often told us in the Pauline Epistles. We abide in Him and can be fruitful (John 15:1-3). We have been brought in Christ to God Himself.

This state of cleansing speaks of a brand new way of life. We are not just sober but walking in the newness of life. All that previously alienated us from God has been taken out of the way. God has given us a Word; He has revealed Himself in Christ (John 1:1-4, 14, 18). When we receive that Word, we are given power to become the sons of God (John 1:12). That Word is the way (John 14:6). That Word is to be loved and followed. We are His disciples, and His commands are our opportunities to show our love and devotion to Him. It, again, is not for us to do His will. We delight in doing so. This is not the sterile motions of keeping steps to perform some mindless will of a god of our own making. This is a real, true, and loving relationship.

The Word of God changes all that formerly kept us from God; our will, our intellect, and our affections. "God be thanked, that ye were the servants of sin, but ye have obeyed from the heart that form of doctrine which was delivered you" (Rom 6:17). We encounter a form of doctrine, the faith of Christ, which enlivens our minds. When encountering the truth of God our will is conquered to obey the gospel. We are made willing in the day of His power (Ps 110). When hearing the faith of Christ, our affections are changed.

We have gone from loving darkness to longing for light. We obey from the heart in the matter of salvation (Rom 10:8-10). It goes from the head to the heart to the hand, as Vance Havner once said. This completes the description of the new creation.

This truth of the gospel is the same when it comes to living a life of righteousness. The bondage of iniquity is broken, and we can now yield to our new Master (Rom 6:16). We now, being reconciled to God, can hear the voice of God, know His will, and follow Him. "My sheep hear my voice, and I know them, and they follow me" (John 10:27). There is delight in taking heed to the Words of God that cleanse our way. We hide it in our hearts that we might not sin against Him in any way. We hide that which we most treasure. The addict will hide his addiction under layers of lies. The new creature will hide the Word of God in their heart. The truth of the Word of God in the believer is just as obvious as the drugs are in the addict. Following Christ is a new way of life. Again, Christ said, "If ye continue in my word, then are ye my disciples indeed; and ye shall know the truth, and the truth shall make you free" (John 8:31, 32). We have there the same elements of the word being spoken, the will with all affection responding, and freedom being experienced.

There is a bonding between us and Christ that has occurred, and it completely changes our relationship to sin. When we encounter Christ, He changes us. We are followers of Christ. That is the true nature of every believer. Christ is the Master, and we are His disciples in terms of our mind. Christ is the Head, and we are His body in the terms of our will. He is the Bridegroom, and we are the Bride in terms of our affections. He has our heads, our hearts, and our hands. We are, as often stated by Paul, in Him. We are in Him and He is in us. We share with Him an intimacy that is unparalleled. Our past is His past, and our future is His future. He is our representative Head. We are set with Him in heavenly places and in Him; we will forever have an audience with God (Eph 2:4-7). He has become bone of our bone, and He has brought us to God (John 14:6). We are forever bonded to Him. In this, there is no condemnation (Rom 8:1, 4). Further, this bond between us and Christ frees us from sin. "For the law of the Spirit of life in Christ Jesus hath made me free from the law of sin and death" (Rom 8:2).

We are something more than simply disciples in a master/student relationship; we are friends. Not only are we friends, we are spoken of in the most intimate of relationships. We are married to Him. He is our Master to instruct our will, our Counselor to instruct our minds, and our Friend or Brother or Spouse to instruct our emotions. This bonding to our Lord keeps us from sin. As long as we are following Christ, we are moving away from sin. Paul argued, when speaking of the temptation to commit sexual sin, that our bond with Christ is sufficient to keep us from the indulgence of sinful pleasures. The same applies to the pleasures enticing us into substances. "Know ye not that your bodies are the members of Christ? shall I then take the members of Christ, and make them the members of an harlot" (1 Cor 6:15)? We, being joined to Christ, cannot join ourselves to sinful things without involving and soiling Him and His holy image (1 Cor 6:13-20). We are for the Lord. We are to be faithful to Him in all things, and every sin is an act of unfaithfulness. With each move away from sin in obedience to Him, we show our love to Him who loved us and washed us from our sin in His own blood (Rev 1:6).

# Necessity # 4

THERE IS ALSO A need to *walk in the Spirit*. The Scriptures call on us to realize that there are two principles at work in us, the flesh and the Spirit of the living God. We have within us that principle of the flesh, which is bent toward the things of this world and the pleasures thereof. This is what is natural to all. However, the follower of Christ has a present reality and experience within them that is contrary to sin. "Walk in the Spirit, and ye shall not fulfil the lust of the flesh" (Gal 5:17). The works of the flesh are not going to stop trying to entice us when we begin to follow Christ. Our following Christ often increases attempted enticement toward evil. The tempter is seeking to devour those among the followers of Christ. The works or lusts of the flesh include all manner of things that are called addictions (Gal 5:19-21). The Christian is promised that they will be the battleground of a war that is fought between these things tempting us and the blessed influence of the Holy Spirit of God within us. "The flesh lusteth against the Spirit, and the Spirit against the flesh: and these are contrary the one to the other: so that ye cannot do the things that ye would" (Gal 5:17). Our own strength is insufficient in winning the war with the flesh. Sobriety, in its true fullness in the Christian life, is the fruit of us yielding ourselves to the Spirit. This bears fruit in our life that is contrary to the works of the flesh (Gal. 5:22, 23). This is the realization of the gospel of Christ in our lives (Gal 5:24). We have a promise that if we walk in the Spirit, the lust of the flesh will not be fulfilled in us.

What does it mean to walk in the Spirit? Walking immediately speaks of fellowship and, in this case, fellowship with God. The first mention of walking in the Bible speaks of the separation of man and God with God walking alone in the garden (Gen 3:8). The next three mentions of walking in the Bible speak of man reconciled in fellowship with God, Enoch and Noah (Gen 5:22,

24, 6:9). Paul then tells us of the role of the Holy Spirit in the renewed fellowship with God. Walking in the Spirit is to enjoy communion with the Father and Son through the Spirit. Walking also speaks of obedience or continuation in a specific way or path. "Ye shall walk in all the ways which the LORD your God hath commanded you . . . " (Deut 5:23). To walk with God in the Spirit one must adhere fully to the direction of God's law. We must not turn to the right hand or left hand if we are to walk in the Spirit. We are to consider the words of God to be right in all things and hate every false way (Ps 119:128). Walking speaks of progression as well. To walk with God in the Spirit is to go through things together with Him in this life. We walk through the valley of the shadow of death and through the fires of temptation because He is with us (Ps 23:4, Isa 43:2). Walking is to know through experience the presence of God as you progress through the troubles of life. Therefore, it is to walk with God in fellowship, within the boundaries of His word, through the troubles of life to your final destination. We add that it is to be at His pace. Two cannot walk together unless they are agreed (Amos 3:3).

Walking requires strength, requiring the necessity of the Spirit. As Christ healed the lame that they may walk through the Spirit, so He by the Spirit enabled us to walk with Him. Walking speaks of the overall direction of one's life. The way we walk is proof of whether or not we have the Spirit of God, which is proof of whether or not we truly know God. We that are saved used to walk in disobedience to God, after the pleasure of our flesh according to the spirit of this world (Eph 2:2, 3). Now we are among those "who walk not after the flesh, but after the Spirit" (Rom 8:1, 4). This is the identity of the saved (Rom 8:5-9).

Nevertheless, there is a sense in which we do not do this perfectly in this life. We are reminded that, if we are to keep ourselves from fulfilling desires of our flesh, we must mindfully walk in the Spirit. This is synonymous with living in and being led by the Spirit (Gal 5:18, 25). Having life and leadership from the Spirit, we now give ourselves to walk fully in Him. This will produce in us fruit that is contrary to the selfish lust that we experienced in our

## PART 2: THE POWER OF THE GOSPEL OVER ADDICTION

lostness and addiction, keeping us from falling into those weaker elements again. Having this fruit is to know the liberty of the Spirit from needing something more to cope and thrive in life (Gal 5:1). We can live free from the influence of our sins, "where the Spirit of the Lord is, there is liberty" (2 Cor 3:17). This is indelibly connected with our following of Christ that we already highlighted. "If ye continue in my word, then are ye my disciples indeed; And ye shall know the truth, and the truth shall make you free" (John 8:31, 32). The condition of continuing in the word of Christ and experiencing freedom from the bondage of sin is connected now to our relationship with the Holy Spirit.

Walking in the Spirit produces fruit in our life that is contrary to sin and selfish desires. We have in this fruit all that the addiction promises, but never can give (Gal 5:22, 23). In the Spirit, we have love. We have the love of God shed abroad or abundantly in our hearts by the Holy Spirit (Rom 5:5). We enter into an experience of love that is past knowledge. We have experienced the love of the cross and the love of the eternal persons of God that are the sum of all love. We have joy. In the presence of God, we have the fullness of joy and pleasures forevermore (Ps 16:11). We have peace. The carnal or flesh-filled mind has nothing but death, but the spiritually-minded is at peace (Rom 8:6). We have peace with God through salvation from sin and shame and the peace of God in the tumultuous circumstances of life (Rom 5:1, Phil 4:6, see Ps 23). We have a tenderness toward others in longsuffering, gentleness, and real goodness after the nature of God shown and experienced in us. We have faith, meekness, and temperance. Whereby we can now walk in faithfulness where once we could not be trusted, we can walk in submission where once we were obstinate, and we can walk in holy constraint in our life where once we caved under every temptation. What a wonderful thought that the Spirit produces in us in the end temperance, the ability to abstain from our addiction!

So, how do we walk in the Spirit? We should first settle on the idea that the Holy Spirit is real. He is a real personal presence. He is God; and when we experience Him, we are experiencing God. He is really in union with all who have trusted Christ and

## NECESSITY # 4

are following Christ. If we are truly Christian, the Spirit is with us and will never leave us. Moreover, we can be filled in a greater way by Him, "be filled with the Spirit" (Eph 5:17). We can pray and have the Spirit in a greater way in our life. "If ye then, being evil, know how to give good gifts unto your children: how much more shall your heavenly Father give the Holy Spirit to them that ask him" (Luke 11:13). This seeking of the empowerment and presence and filling of the Spirit are necessary to walking in Him. There is something more of God we can have. In fact, we are as godly as we truly want to be. We have as much of God as we truly desire. If we truly want God, instead of our sins, we need to desire more of the influence of the Spirit in our life. We walk in Him and, in doing so, separate ourselves from the sin of our addiction.

There are some synonyms of the Spirit, in other contexts of Scripture that shed more light on the meaning of walking in the Spirit. Walking in the Spirit is in another place called walking in newness of life (Rom 6:4). The context of that truth is living out the gospel of Christ in our life. We are dead with Christ. We are buried with Christ. We now live by Christ through His resurrection. We are fully identified with Him. Therefore, we do not continue in sin. We are free to serve Him and yield our lives to Him. Our lives are made new, and we walk in that reality. Such we do, when we walk in the Spirit. We walk also by faith (2 Cor 5:7). To walk by faith is to walk according to a rule or pattern (Rom 4:12). Our faith is that substance and evidence that we have been given of God to believe (Heb 11:1). This, therefore, speaks of being faithful to that which God speaks, like the prophet Samuel walked according to the heart and mind of God (1 Sam 2:35). We turn from walking by our own sight or understanding to walk according to what God speaks. The Holy Spirit gives us the truth of Christ and, when we walk in that faith, we walk in Him. We walk worthy of our vocation (Eph 4:1-3). This speaks of the kind and gentle and loving behavior that we have as those who are servants and therefore representatives of Christ. The wicked servant, proving himself to not be a true servant, smote his fellow servants and ate and drank with drunkards (Matt 24:49). When we have a churlish spirit before men, we are not walking as servants of the Lord or in His Spirit. We walk circumspectly (Eph 5:15). That means to walk carefully, careful to obey all things and careful to guard ourselves against all disobedience. We walk in honesty (Eph 5:2). The context there is one of self-sacrifice after the pattern of Christ. It is to give ourselves for others. It is to give ourselves in love to a life of living and holy bodily sacrifice in worship to our God (Rom 12:1). We walk honestly (Rom 13:13). We walk without hypocrisy. We live our life in genuine and unfeigned love. We walk in truth (2 John 1:4). We confine what we do and do not do to what is expressed in the Word of God. We walk in wisdom (Col 4:8). We seek to apply the instruction and knowledge of the Word of God to our daily decisions. We walk in the light (1 John 1:7). We live our life in personal fellowship with God. We walk in the presence of God, in the light of what He has shared with us about Himself (Ps 89:15). We walk in love in self-sacrifice after the pattern of Christ (Eph 5:2).

The measure to which we do these things is the measure to which we are filled with the Spirit. Moreover, if we are filled with the Spirit, we are far from being drunk with wine (Eph 5:18). This is the very Spirit that filled Christ in His earthly walk (Luke 4:1, 14). Isaiah prophesied of our Lord, "the spirit of the Lord shall rest upon him, the spirit of wisdom and understanding, the spirit of counsel and might, the spirit of knowledge and of the fear of the Lord . . . " (Isa 11:2). This is the only power whereby we can walk in the steps of the Lord (Zech 4:6).

These things are all indicative or what walking in the Spirit is and how we do it. Further, to understand how to walk in the Spirit, we must finally understand what keeps the presence of the Spirit from being enjoyed. There are sins against the Spirit. There are three things in the Scriptures identified as such. They all relate one to another interconnectedly; and when committing one, we find that we also commit the other two.

First, we can sin against the Spirit by resisting the Spirit. "Ye stiffnecked and uncircumcised in heart and ears, ye do always resist the Holy Ghost" (Acts 7:51). In its extreme form, it is the sin for which there is no forgiveness, the blasphemy of the Holy Ghost

(Matt 12:31, 32). That sin is resisting the Spirit to the point of actual positive repudiation and speaking against the demonstrated work of the Spirit. It is in a final way to declare the Spirit as evil as it declares the truth of Christ. There is a resisting that comes to the point of no return, which point is known to God alone. There are lesser forms of resisting that all men are guilty. Resisting is described as being stiff-necked, refusing like a mule to be turned at the direction of the reigns. It is described as being uncircumcised in heart and ears, to have a heart and ears that will not be set apart from its sin (Zech 7:11-13). To continue in such is to fall into the sin of presumption for which there is no sacrifice or atonement, which answers to the blasphemy of the Holy Ghost (Heb 10:26-31, Num 15:1-31, as opposed to ignorant sins that, when their guilt is known before God, will turn and trust in a substitutionary sacrifice). Resisting is the natural state of all who are lost or dead in sins. Men in their natural state reject the authority of God in their sinful ignorance. They have done so since the fall. Human history as a whole, as well as the Jewish history described in the context of the martyr Stephen (Acts 7), testify to the rebellion of mankind against the commandments of God.

Those who have begun to follow Christ through the renewing of the Holy Ghost (Titus 3:5, see John 3:3-7 regarding regeneration or the new birth), have come into a new relationship with God and His Word. The Holy Spirit is the Spirit of truth (John 15:26, 16:13). In fact, seeing that He moved men to write the Scriptures (2 Pet 1:21), He is truth (1 John 5:6). Before we became followers of Christ, He convinced us and witnessed to us the truth of Christ (John 16:7, 8). It is through this sanctifying work that we believed the truth and became followers of Christ (2 Thess 2:13, 1 Pet 1:22). The Spirit of truth does not stop His work once we are born again. He guides us into all truth (John 16:13). The Holy Spirit is our guide after Christ and the Word of God and the commandments of God are the means. "For the commandment is a lamp; and the law is light; and reproofs of instruction are the way of life" (Prov 6:23).

The disciple, when hearing the Word of God, becomes aware that there are yet areas of his life that are not yet submitted to

Christ. The Holy Spirit is constantly moving us from our own sinful self-will and self-authority to bring us under the authority of God and to do His will. When we pull against the Spirit of truth, we are resisting His work in our lives. For instance, the Word of God may confront us with the command to submit to every ordinance of man. Through hearing that command, the Spirit pulls you in toward applying that truth in your life. He convicts you of breaking the speed limit and running stop signs. The Spirit leads us to take the Word of God and live out the truth of it. Resisting the Spirit is to pull toward the lie. It is to deny the truth of God in our behavior. It is unfaithfulness or infidelity toward God who would have us live according to His truth.

We get a picture of a petulant child pulling away from a parent guiding them to bed. The fearful truth though is even greater. If we resist God, we are resisting all power. The story of Ananias and Sapphira shows us the fearful aspect of resisting the Spirit of truth (Acts 5:1-11). They promised to give the price of a sale of property to the church, but then they ended up gaining more than they thought they would get. Wanting to appear to be giving all, while enjoying the extra that they had promised for themselves, they went about to deceive. They decided to lie to the church and give only part of what they promised. Peter told them directly that they had lied to God; they had lied to the Holy Ghost. Their behavior was the opposite of the truth of God who would have us in all things to live honestly (Heb 13:18). To walk with the Spirit is to allow Him to guide us into all truth.

Secondly, to sin against the Spirit is to grieve the Spirit. "And grieve not the holy Spirit of God, whereby ye are sealed unto the day of redemption" (Eph 4:30). Where resisting the Spirit speaks of our individual relationship to the Word of God, grieving the Spirit speaks of our relationship to the church (see the whole of chapter 4 of Ephesians). The Spirit leads us to purity through obedience "unto unfeigned love of the brethren..." that we "... love one another with a pure heart fervently . . . " (1 Pet 1:22). The Spirit is known as our Comforter (John 14:26, 15:26, 16:7). He comforts His people and leads us to do the same through Him. He sheds love abroad in our hearts (Rom. 5:5). The first fruit He brings forth in our life is love (Gal 5:22). Paul said, "If there be therefore any consolation in Christ, if any comfort of love, if any fellowship of the Spirit, if any bowels and mercies, Fulfil ye my joy, that ye be likeminded, having the same love, being of one accord, of one mind" (Phil 2:1, 2). The Spirit of God is among the people of God making overtures of love and is grieved when that love is not expressed. Like a spurned lover, He will withdraw from us if He is grieved. We saw that pictured with the indifferent bride in Song of Solomon, who selfishly would not rise in love for her Bridegroom (Song 5:1-6).

The context of the fourth chapter of Ephesians speaks of the need to give up anger, selfishness, wrath, and malice. Instead, we are to forgive one another and give one to another. The Holy Spirit promotes love and unity between those who are born of God. It is an offense to God for there to be discord among brethren (Prov 6:16-19). The Christian cannot walk in love with God without walking in love with God's people. This is not a call for compromise on biblical truth in the name of false unity, but it is a call for a loving church fellowship and care for Christians God brings along our way. We treat Christ the same way we treat Christians (Matt 25:34-45). If we are to walk with the Spirit, we must walk in love and mercy with the people of God (Eph 5:1, 2).

Finally, we sin against the Spirit by quenching the Spirit. "Quench not the Spirit" (1 Thess 5:19). Resisting the Spirit speaks of our relationship to the Word of God and grieving the Spirit speaks of our relationship to God's people, this speaks of our relationship to the work of God. The Spirit of God is convincing the world of the sin and of the truth of Christ (John 16:6-9). He is the Spirit of truth and the Comforter and now is fire (Matt 3:11). Christ came to send fire on this earth, and we are to help kindle it (Luke 12:49). The Holy Spirit is the catalyst (Acts 2:3). To quench something is to extinguish or attempt to extinguish. It is to stop the work. There is no intention in God to contain the fire of His consuming presence. The fire never says it is enough (Prov 30:16). When we pray for the name of God to be hallowed, we mean for it to be hallowed everywhere (Matt 6:9). This is the missionary spirit. Preach the gospel everywhere, that His name may be glorified. There is no other valid reason to preach the gospel. God wants us to be light that He may be glorified.

If we quench this fire, we stop the work. The Spirit strives with men, and we are to strive. We can quench the fire by covering it with water or earth or by removing fuel. We can abuse the truth of the gospel with our behavior or discourage the work by our neglect. We can, by selfish behavior, make the gospel obnoxious. We can, by our neglect of the work, make it appear without efficacy. The context of the command to not quench the Spirit provides clues. We quench the Spirit when we fail to rejoice in God in our lives (1 Thess 5:16). We quench the Spirit by failing to pray and demonstrate our full dependency on God for all things (1 Thess 5:17). We quench the Spirit when we fail to be thankful to God in all our circumstances, recognizing His presence and loving care (1 Thess 5:18). We quench the Spirit when we fail to love the Word of God as it is proclaimed rightly, even when it comes from sources that cause personal contention (1 Thess 5:20). There is no room for a party spirit in the work of God. We quench the Spirit when we fail to study the Word of God carefully and hold only to those ideas that prove good and true to the Word of God (1 Thess 5:21). We quench the Spirit when we do not walk circumspectly, avoiding even the appearance of sin and hypocrisy, which would turn people from the gospel (1 Thess 5:22). If we are to walk in the Spirit, we are to be sensitive to the work He is doing in the spread of the gospel and how our actions and inactions affect it.

# Necessity # 5

CONSIDER YET ANOTHER CONNECTING truth; we need to *grow in knowledge*. "But grow in grace, and in the knowledge of our Lord and Savior Jesus Christ" (2 Pet 3:18). Walking involves progress. There is repentance in leaving something behind. There is love in following. There is trust in the end to which you head. Moreover, all throughout, there is progress. We get further from where we were, closer to where we are going, and more intimate with the one with whom we go. We may call this progress growth. We grow into the stature of Christ through the sanctifying work of the Spirit. When we were children we behaved as children, but when we became adults we stopped behaving as children (1 Cor 13:11). However, there is a point that we can reach, which the Scriptures call perfection or rather maturity, and that perfection is charity (1 Cor 13:10, 13).

There is a childish selfishness in addiction. It is a sad thing to see a young adult engaged in it, but it is even more tragic to see a middle aged or elderly person acting in the same way. To grow up in the knowledge of Christ is to put on charity and put away childish selfishness. We can go from having new life in Christ (John 3:3), to being a babe desiring the sincere milk of the word of God (1 Pet 2:2), to being little children assured of their forgiveness and their place as God's children (1 John 2:12, 13), to being young men victorious and strong in the Word of God (1 John 2:13, 14), to fathers of deeper fellowship with God (1 John 2:13, 14), to the aged who are examples of faith and charity (Titus 2:2). The growth or progress of faith is always toward conforming us to the perfect image of Christ, growing up into Him (Rom 8:29, Eph 4:15). This is not sinless perfection, for we always are to have a sensitivity toward sin in our lives (1 John 1:8, 10), but a maturity in Christ whereby we walk as He walked (1 John 2:6).

There was a greater principle by which He lived and that principle is known as charity. When we grow or progress into this principle of life through the fear of God, the discipleship of Christ, and union with the Spirit, we open up the possibility of the full experience of victory; "if these things be in you, and abound, they make you that ye shall neither be barren nor unfruitful in the knowledge of our Lord Jesus Christ . . . if ye do these things, ye shall never fall . . . " (2 Pet 1:8, 10). There is something that can be done to insulate from relapse. Relapse may be part of treatment, but the gospel is not treatment. The gospel is the embracing of the truth. The promises embraced urge the believer to progress toward the greater end and in doing so to not be mindful of that left behind (Heb 11:13-16, Phil 3:13, 14).

The context of this growth is the fellowship of the people of God. We build one another up in the faith of Christ (Jude 1:20, Eph 4:11-16). Those who forsake the community of faith keep themselves from growing up fully into Christ. Peter described this growth best, giving the promise that it would make it to where we would never fall. This growth begins with receiving grace and peace from God, experiencing His divine power through knowledge of Him, trusting the gospel of Christ (John 1:12), believing His great promises toward us, and being in communion with His divine nature (2 Pet 1:2-4). This is all synonymous with the salvation we have in Christ. It is simply known as our faith (2 Pet 1:5). We can add to that in our growth and progress in the faith. We can build our life on a sure foundation (Eph 2:19-22, Matt 7:24-29, 1 Cor 3:9-16).

We can add virtue to our faith (2 Pet 1:5). Rather, let your faith produce in you virtue. This is moral character, which is subjection generally to all areas of life to the rule of God. It is not something you can have separate from faith, but rather in addition to your faith and growing out from it. We allow our faith to produce in us moral actions. This moral purity was the very power in Christ that healed men (Luke 6:19). It was the power in Christ that changed others. Our faith is of no value if it does not produce the works of faith in us (Jas 2:17). Do not let your faith be idle, but allow it to dictate every action. We then allow

## NECESSITY # 5

our faith to build further knowledge (2 Pet 1:5). Having already the knowledge of Him in salvation, we go on to allow our faith to show us more of Him that we may follow Him closer. Paul longed for greater knowledge of Christ (Phil 3:10). Knowing the person and work of Christ allows us to follow Him closer, being changed into His very image. We then add to that temperance. This is self or rather scriptural discipline (1 Cor 9:25). Learn how to let your faith control your behavior, correct you when you are erring, and equip you to do right (2 Tim. 3:16, 17). Let your faith add patience (2 Pet. 1:6). Let your faith work endurance in you. Let it bring you through each trouble and give you experience in grace by continuing faithful through each trial (Rom 5:3-5). Let your faith add godliness to you (2 Pet. 1:6). Let your faith work in you to the point that you do all things with a conscience toward God, His glory, and His presence in full dependency upon Him. That is the meaning of the term godly and the absence of that is what it means to be ungodly. We then allow our faith to add brotherly kindness. Kindness is to act in a way to meet a need of another. Let our faith cause us to act in kindness to a brother in need (Jas 2:15, 16). Let your faith build in you kindness toward any that can be called your brother in Christ. Let forgiveness and mercy reign through grace and learn to speak and act kindly to those God has put in your way. Once you have done that, you let your faith add charity (2 Pet 1:7). Charity is the acts of love (1 Cor 13). It is the perfection of Christ (Col 3:14). Let the love of Christ grow from you toward all that are in your way. When you grow up to that point, you will never again fall into sinful behavior again.

More can be said about keeping you from sin, but you are going to have to start following Christ to learn. The life of faith is broader than what can be contained in this treatise. It is broader than doing steps mechanically over and over. It is about a true relationship with God, and that is hard to explain; it has to be lived.

Therefore, I will end my meager rambling to a few more short words. What you need to be free from addiction is a supernatural miracle to change you. That is true no matter the sin. This comes only from the mercy of God through Christ and leads into a life of worship (Rom 12:1, 2). If this miraculous work begins in you, the same power will continue until the end (Phil 1:6). Seek that work. Seek it in Christ until you know you have it. Call on Him until you know He has heard you. He will have mercy on whom He wills, so go to Him (Rom 9:15). Once He grants you faith and repentance, that work will never stop. There is power in the gospel, seek it. It can make addiction a description of what you once were and not a present power in your life (1 Cor 6:6-10). It can give you powerful new desires after God and the things of God. There is power there. There is power in the conviction of the Spirit to convince us (John 16:13). There is power in the word of God to search us (Heb 4:12). There is power in repentance worked in us by the preaching of Truth to move us toward the living and holy God (2 Cor 7:8-11). There is power in the faith of Christ to give us new life (Gal 2:20). This is what you can have in Christ. On the other hand, you can keep chasing your sin to your death and eternal destruction. Seek Christ while He may be found.

# Appendix: Dealing with Rock Bottom

A WORD SHOULD BE said about the idea of hitting "rock bottom" when dealing with the compulsion toward substance abuse. However, we will not use the term "rock bottom" in the same way the treatment community uses it. When they speak of "rock bottom," they speak of a time when the addict comes to the absolute end of themselves, when they come to their lowest possible point. It is the crisis, which causes them to finally seek a high power to help them. The big problem with this conventional wisdom is that it tends to create an imaginary subjective boundary that one never knows if they reach. Rock bottom could be waking up in their own vomit for some, going to jail for others, or a near death experience for others. Since it cannot be concretely defined, "rock bottom" means whatever the addict wants it to mean. Moreover, as long as the addict still is gaining something from the experience of using drugs or alcohol, they are free to define "rock bottom" as something that they have not yet reached. Therefore, they are emboldened to continue in their way no matter how terrible the consequences of their actions are. There are always further depths of depravity that an addict can go into. Ultimately, they can die still believing that the high is a good trade-off for the consequences. Real "rock bottom" is eternal destruction in the reality of hell, but by then it is too late. One should not wait for a fictitious point to turn from their sins to the living God.

There is a sense in which each sinner needs to come to themselves, but that has little or nothing to do with whether or not the circumstances around them become sufficiently deplorable. Did God use the circumstances of the prodigal son to spur him to go to the Father? Yes! Nevertheless, Matthew and Zacchaeus came in full material wealth and Cornelius in political prosperity received Christ. What is needed is for one to come to themselves in the sense of seeing their spiritual poverty as sinners and the abundance of grace that we could have if we went to God and He received us.

The "rock bottom" that is our subject now is not that which brings men to Christ, but that "rock bottom" that we seem to experience while we walk with Christ. There are temptations to go back to the weak and beggarly elements from which Christ has made us free. There will be times that we will deal with despondency and despair. There may be times that we do not understand the suffering and anguish we experience. In the world, we shall have tribulation (John 16:33). We must be prepared to go through the tribulation.

David wrote two psalms speaking of despair (Ps 42 & 43). In those Psalms, David reveals a heart-wrenching take of being at "rock bottom." In those Psalms, David goes back and forth from disparity to faith. There are two choruses in these Psalms that describe the believer in crisis reaching out to God. The first chorus is stated but once, "Why art thou cast down, O my soul? and why art thou disquieted in me? hope thou in God: for I shall yet praise him for the help of his countenance" (Ps 42:5). The second chorus is repeated twice, once in each Psalm, only slightly varied from the first chorus. "Why art thou cast down, O my soul? and why art thou disquieted within me? hope thou in God: for I shall yet praise him, who is the health of my countenance, and my God" (Ps 42:11, 43:5). The choruses tie the two Psalms together. In this singular theme, where does the believer turn when they are brought to their lowest possible point?

It is a given fact that those who trust God may experience times of despair. The repeated nature of the chorus indicates that one may repeatedly struggle with despair. Two things stick out as descriptive of the turmoil of suffering. There is the term "cast down," which describes the hopelessness one may come to feel. To be cast down is to be laid prostrate, to be brought to the lowest point, or rather to hit "rock bottom." The term is used for the judgement of Satan, for instance. Then there is the word *disquieted*. This word speaks of stress and anxiety. It tells of being full of disharmony, noise, and clamoring. We can think of being bombarded with the sound of a

## APPENDIX: DEALING WITH ROCK BOTTOM

child banging on piano keys. It is to have no peace of mind. The Christian is not immune to such a state. Christ in His passion in the garden of Gethsemane, Christ cried out, "My soul is exceeding sorrowful, even unto death: tarry ye here, and watch with me" (Matt 26:38). It is at this very time that He told us to watch with Him and told us that we could enter into temptation if we do not watch (Matt 26:41). If we walk with Christ, we may walk through Gethsemane from time to time. It is a dangerous time.

Just as Christ cried out "why" when He bore our sins, so when we bear His righteousness we may sometimes cry out as the psalmist did, "Why!" The question here is not why these things are happening, for the gospel tells us why they happen (if Christ suffered, so shall we carry a cross), but the question is why are we so cast down and disquieted. Ultimately, we know it to be a matter of our "soul." Our inward man is cast down, our spirits. We are brought low and want to give up. Why? It is a question seeking and reaching out for God.

So much can bring us down in life. In these two Psalms, David goes back and forth speaking of the things that disquieted him and trying to encourage himself through those things. The disquieting things included failing health, mocking religious enemies, and deceitful and unjust enemies. However, despite the greatness of the trial and even the darkness of the language, the psalmist speaks of hope. The world has an inferior version of what David does in these Psalms. Cognitive behavioral therapy, trusting only in the power of human reasoning, directs people to change the way they think in order to direct their behavior in times of turmoil. Here, David rises above the humanism of cognitive behavioral therapy to embrace biblical thinking after and through God. The believer in times of great trial can find relief in God alone. Affliction can be carried with joy. Enemies can be faced with courage. We have a false idea that God will not put on us more than we can bear, when all that we face in good times and bad, is more than we can bear. One preacher rightly said that without God he could not even tie our shoes. The trial is meant to show us this truth. His grace alone is sufficient. Therefore, we read these Psalms and engage in biblical cognitive therapy. We journey from despair to hope, from "rock bottom" to heaven itself. To do so we will look at three key words in the chorus; *hope*, *help*, and *health*.

First, the Psalms are an encouragement toward *hope*. Despite being cast down and disquieted, David tells himself in all three choruses to "hope thou in God . . . ." He talks to himself to tell himself to place his hope only in God. The meat of the hope is also stated in each chorus, the faith found in the statement "for I shall yet praise Him . . . ." Despite the darkness of the present situation, he reminded himself of the hope he had and the expectation of future praise. How can he do this? The clues are in the Psalms themselves. Vance Havner compared texts like this to sample pages to a great book or crumbs to the whole cake. Despite the notes of anguish and despair, David kept turning back to things He knew of God. Those crumbs caused him to, time and time again, ask why he was even cast down and to encourage hope that he shall yet praise God again. The greatest preaching you will ever hear is the preaching you do to yourself from the Word of God in the deepest moments of despair. It is the foretaste of glory as Fanny Crosby once sang. Consider the crumbs of the text.

First, he reminds himself that in God alone he can find all he needs. "As the hart panteth after the water brooks, so panteth my soul after thee, O God. My soul thirsteth for God, for the living God: when shall I come and appear before God" (Ps 42: 1, 2)? The panting is a result of the trial. The deer or hart ran quickly from danger to find itself parched and unable to go forward. It longs and pants, not for the luxury of wine but for the necessity of water. God is life, and His presence is life giving. The thirst that I now experience can quickly end if I drink from Him. The death I feel can flee from the living God, the resurrection and life. The end question for our trial is when we may appear before God. The presence of His glory is all we need. In addition, we know it is not a question of if but rather when we shall appear there before Him.

Secondly, there is the experience we have had in His fellowship. "I had gone with the multitude, I went with them to the house of God, with the voice of joy and praise, with a multitude that kept holyday" (Ps 42:4). The common experience of every true believer in Christ is the joy of corporate worship. Where two or three are gathered together in the name of Christ, there He is. Remembering the joy of going to where God is with God's people is a great encouragement in the Lord. Remembering how we have praised our Lord with the voice of joy and praise is a great inducement to the flaming of hope that we shall one day do it again.

Thirdly, we may recall His previous victories that He has wrought in our experience. "O my God, my soul is cast down within me: therefore will I remember thee from the land of Jordan, and of the Hermonites, from the hill Mizar" (Ps 42:6). What was the land of Jordan but that place where God parted the river to make a way for His people to cross on dry land to possess His promises (Josh 4)? Who were the Hermonites but the remnant of giants God gave us victory over (Deut 3:6-11). Even in our lowest state, as Christians, we know of victory in Christ. Our sins were removed, we have obtained promises of eternal life, we have faced giants through Christ and have won ground. We are not what we used to be because of Him.

Fourthly, we consider His faithfulness even in darkness. "Yet the Lord will command his lovingkindness in the day time, and in the night his song shall be with me, and my prayer unto the God of my life (Ps 42:8)." If there is help in darkness, it can only come from God. All men know that intuitively. That is why they call to God in the most helpless of circumstances. However, we that know Him know that in the night He can give songs. He is a God of grace or lovingkindness. He commands goodness toward His people. Moreover, He is the God of my life. We stand in a confident position even in darkness before a faithful God.

Fifthly, we consider our relationship to God, that is our relationship to Him through grace. There was a time that we were without God (Eph. 2:12). Even in despair, the language of the Christian is one of possessive and relational context when speaking of God. He is "God my rock" (Ps. 42:9) and is constantly being called "my God" and said by our enemies to be "thy God." He is God of "my strength" (Ps 43:2). He is the deepest supply of my needs. We are wholly His dependents. Then there is even a crescendo of relationship language, He is "God my exceeding joy" (Ps 43:4). There is a deep reality of relationship that we now have with the eternal God. He is ours, we are His, and His banner over us is love (Song 2:4, 16). We call Him, Father; Christ we call Husband and Brother; the Holy Ghost, we call Comforter. There is an eternal love relationship between the persons of the eternal Godhead, and we have been invited to have a real part in that.

Sixthly, we consider that He is the true judge. "Judge me, O God, and plead my cause against an ungodly nation: O deliver me from the deceitful and unjust man" (Ps 43:1). The righteous of this world are maligned by the wicked and persecuted by the world. There is no sure place of judgement. However, God is the righteous Judge, and we call upon Him who knows all things truly. His cause is our cause, and He will in truth plead it for us.

Lastly, we consider that He can supply our deepest need. "O send out thy light and thy truth: let them lead me; let them bring me unto thy holy hill, and to thy tabernacles. Then will I go unto the altar of God, unto God my exceeding joy: yea, upon the harp will I praise thee, O God my God" (Ps 43:3, 4). His light can lead us. His truth can comfort us. They can give us the leadership we need. They can bring us to the altar of God for the worship we need to express. They can bring true joy. They can produce true singing.

More crumbs could be found in these Psalms. These though are sufficient to induce us to hope more in God even in times of despair.

Once we grasp our hope again firmly in the person of God, we move from hope to *help*, "for I shall yet praise him for the help of his countenance" (Ps 42:5. With hope comes help. Our help comes from the Lord, which made heaven and earth (Ps 121:1, 2). The highlight in this text now is His countenance. It speaks of one's facial expression and speaks more deeply here of a personal and intimate presence. The root of the English word means to contain and speak of the demeanor and behavior of something, which directs to the face as the expression of emotion. The blessing to the Nazarite from the priest was thus, "The Lord bless thee,

## APPENDIX: DEALING WITH ROCK BOTTOM

and keep thee: The Lord make his face shine upon thee, and be gracious unto thee: The Lord lift up his countenance upon thee, and give thee peace" (Num 6:24-26). It is that very blessing here that is being evoked. It is the light and truth of God that was evoked later in the Forty-third psalm (Ps 4:6). It is the strength of God we already highlighted (Ps 11:7). It is the exceeding joy we already exclaimed (Ps 21:6). It was the glory that Moses longed to see (Exod 33:18). Sin hid it from man, as they hid from God in the garden. However, now we have the presence of God in Christ. "For God, who commanded the light to shine out of darkness, hath shined in our hearts, to give the light of the knowledge of the glory of God in the face of Jesus Christ" (2 Cor 4:6). God has indeed laid our help on one that is mighty (Ps 89:19). There is no problem in our life that we cannot find help from the knowledge of the presence of Christ in our lives.

With our hope comes our help, and with our help comes our *health*. Twice in these Psalms, the phrase is repeated, "for I shall yet praise him, who is the health of my countenance, and my God" (Ps 42:11, 43:5). When the presence of Christ is known, it heals. Moses had his face shine after knowing the presence of the glory of God (Exod 34:29-33). There is a noticeable change in the person that has been with Jesus (Acts 4:13). We can seek health through many avenues. Nevertheless, true health can only come from the Great Physician. He who healed the sick, cast out devils, and had demoniacs sitting at His feet can change you in your lowest state. With hope comes help and with help comes health.

www.ingramcontent.com/pod-product-compliance
Lightning Source LLC
Chambersburg PA
CBHW071200090426
42736CB00012B/2395